HOMO SAPIENCE

Existence Defined

Joseph II

Matador
5 Weir Road
Kibworth Beauchamp
Leicester LE8 0LQ UK
Tel: 0116 279 2299
Email: books@troubador.co.uk
Web: www.troubador.co.uk/matador

ISBN 9781848762237

A Cataloguing-in-Publication (CIP) catalogue record for this book
is available from the British Library.

Typeset in 11pt Garamond by Troubador Publishing Ltd, Leicester, UK

Matador is an imprint of Troubador Publishing Ltd

*Dedicated to
Christopher and Allan
my pride and glory*

CONTENTS

HOMO SAPIENCE

Existence Defined

A WAILING SCREAM THAT REFUSES
TO BE CUT OUT OF A DREAM
(Maltese language)

(Imjassar b'xi dieqa 'nfittex is-sliem
indur lejn is sema w 'nhabbat il bibien
nhares lejn Alla, lejn id dnub, lejn ix-xemx
indur fuqhi nnifshi w 'nsib li ma hemmx
la hena la fama la biedu, la tmiem,
imhasseb jien wahdi 'ngerfex gol holqien
midrus f'din il morsa mahkuma biz zmien
f' sistema mffassla bla' ebda qisien
Ingawdi, nisghar nahdem w ingorr
Gewwa din il magna li tibni w tholl
Inzomm dik it trejqa li taghder u thenn
ghax taht id dell taghha sejjer nistkenn
mel' ngharbel lil abjad lil iswed w lil griz
Sabiex minn mohhi intafhi kull piz
inkun aktar ghaqli, izjed bizell w onest
Sabiex fl ahhar ezami nisperra nkun lest.
Inzomm dawn it traversi li fuqhom m'hemmx kejl
Sakemm il gurnata tinbidel mal lejl.
    Il harsa ta ommhi w tbissimmha tax xih
Ser nerga ingawdhi meta nsib il nistrieh.
Flimkien m'ohthi, huthi qrabathi w il hbieb
Nergghu' ninaghqdu meta jinghalqhu l'bibien.)

2

TO – OUR LADY OF SORROWS

My dearest Lady of Sorrows
You gave me your days for my tomorrow.
Made me big, strong and wise
By your toil, love and sacrifice.
You invested in me through your beleives
Well aware of the futur greives
Waiting and slaving for all of us
Never waivered away from the cross
In return I trampled over your name
And though its late I'm still ashamed
So dearest mother my truest friend
Tis most unfair if it should all ends
Lost or discarded in any vile manner
Without thanking the best Mother.
So Father, please help me compose
Words of graceful thanks towards my
dearest 'Mother of Sorrows.'

Extract From Nostradamus, Quadrant III.XC III

'Le divin verbe donra a la substance,
Comprins ciel,terre, or occult au laict mystique:
Corp, ame esprit ayant toute puissance,
Tant soubs ses pied comme au siege celique.

Words of divine structure, composed out of physical and pensive
formats would furnish out a spiritual font that would be
supported upon logics and stated over current events.

HOMO SAPIENCE

Introduction

A physical impulse has directed me in order to write what my pensive mentality had directed me to do before I even had got hold of a pen to perform these sorts of texts. My 'being' has been aware about these details through the 'entity ' of my 'person' and all of these sorts of existing codes would consequently be scrolled out of my own kind of a 'self' that is called 'me'. A kind of a board is set in order to compose out this frame of existence if it is ever meant 'to be' versed out by 'us'.

If 'to be' or 'not to be' is the logical process that is managed out by this system thus it follows that our sorts of modern kinds of computers machines are trailing behind us and not the other way around. Since we are ahead of these machines that are helping us to plan and program our different kinds of schedules than these contraptions are nothing new to us. This computing aspect that delivers out information through deleted frames of bytes is a mediocre system when compared with our kinds of existing minds.

A clear example over this conduct is the discovery of the image form of the 'zero' that contains no sort of an amount but has been currently utilized in order to relate values to be counted out into 'tenfold'. Should this 'imaged' 'form' had been discarded in the same manner as those kinds of computing module do, then our calculating kind of capacity would have remained backward 'tenfold' of what it is at this present stage. Other analogue comparisons in the same style as this unconventional mode have shaken us and made us aware that our kind of living is not the same as 'existing'.

Our existing forms that had spearheaded towards specific aims of productivity are sending out clear signs and messages that sustainability is a vital issue that could not be discarded or ignored out from our lives. These forms of shock waves always makes us aware that we are not machines or computer that would produce outwards what they had been fed inwards.

These angles and aspects makes us realize and recognize that existing and living are wide apart and are transformed and revolved for us to be promoted and evolved from their own sorts of source and resources. Over these types of credentials was 'Homo Sapience' awarded the honor and the title of the 'Man who knows'.

A nature of a balanced form can produce a stable conduct in order to be promoted towards a higher sphere, whilst only through unconventional modes could any form be verified in order to actually ' be'.
Living is 'framed' into this particular existing 'case' that we could be able to recognize and discover if we are able to diagnose it in a detached mode.

These sorts of existing 'logistics, statistics of nature form' are all factors over which we conduct our lives and in return they would always leave upon us impacts of different sorts of impressions over which we could relate them out backwards whenever we delve further more inside them.

By means of a rotary process our nature forms could

either revolve along over their modes or could be caught inside their various folds and so would seize to live by being recycled prematurely.

These existing factors consist of 'time/space, relativity, polarity and matter' all of which could be managed or gauged out from their own contents.

All these kinds of existing forms could be explained out from their own types of resources that they own.

Through this process we could divulge out what is currently being done, whilst out from their sources we could be aware about this sort of an existing sphere. Through this revolving system could be scrolled out what had been done and consequently could be projected out what is being expected to happen next.

Our kind of knowledge has managed to gain an edge of an advantage over these kinds of nature forms out of their own sorts of contents.

At this current stage we are well equipped and fully furnished to grade out these nature forms out from their own sorts of potentials. We have managed to gather enough 'knowledge' and therefore must be 'aware' about a frame of 'wisdom' that we are currently imposing and directing over this quadrant bench.

These sorts of knowledge and wisdom are forms of tools and utilities that sustain and support our kind of a nature in order 'to be' in this existing sphere just like everything else around us.

A sane mind as well as a healthy body are important but cannot ever be considered out as 'being' our own kind of a complete 'entity' of a 'self' in their 'personalities' that are all characterized by 'nature forms'.

They are just instruments and tools that are used and

utilized for an aim and purpose that is being directed and indicated out by and through 'us'. We are consequently managing these existing forms that are providing us with information about them as well as about their various kinds of sources and resources that they contain. We tend to lean on them but they would never enable us to be upgraded or evolved if we stay motionless and flow along into their stream.

Our potentials had been upgraded when the existing system of 'cause and effect' was harnessed and put at bay.

When humanity was detached and isolated out from this current trend and managed to compose a purpose out from these cause and effect events, then knowledge was segregated and awareness was instated that took control of existing forms that were regulated out by our 'lives'.

Over this spherical conduct were promoted out genetic features and upon this aspect was graded the intelligence that must have been possessed and regulated out by 'Homo Sapience'.

Wisdom and knowledge evolved and rotated into us by motivation that were steered out from a 'cause and effect' into a diagonal process of concepts and perceptions twinned with forms of images.

This conduct is fashioned out in a sustainable manner over its own kind of merit whenever it is being framed out into our own minds.

Acts, deeds, and all sorts of performances that are staged out have got to be supported out by whatever is situated in this existing sphere here. This rotary process is carried out through a past existing sphere towards a future programmed life that is planned out by 'us' in a detached manner that is aloft from a cause and effect that is revolving here.

Our nature kinds evolve over this conduct, whilst our existence rotates over this computed mode of a static format that is regulated out by whatever had been logged into it. This is a direct line of perception that centers over our physical and pensive kinds of qualities that we have and possess but they could never be considered or even regarded out as being any one of 'us'.

The ways and the manners of how we physically and pensively operate our system is managed and directed out by an analogue manner that is exercised out by all sorts of nature forms, the only difference is that we regulate them and not the other way round.

Information about nature is gathered through awareness by our sensual conducts of 'digestion, audition, feeling and screening' whilst through 'reflections, applications, projections and inverting' we are able to model out thoughts. This diagonal process could be imaged out into any feature, whilst imagination could be composed out into any amount of information that we might verse towards a framework of thoughts out of these physical and pensive nature forms that we might compose.

By means of these modes we could develop, evolve, revolve or verse out forms and by their own kinds of means we could contest, test, protest or accept any item that is, or had been staged before or after them as well.

These sorts of paths, lane, tracks or highways might direct and convey our nature forms in order to travel towards any style that we might 'conceive' or perceive'. These kinds of journeys might transport us along routes ranging from straight to crooked, and then might be curled and get twisted up into an adjacent conduct of an analogue mode that might lodge us over any sphere that we could imagine around this cyclic stage.

These spheres would always contain a type of an environment that would have established out their kinds of habitats over a cause and effect role.

These galaxies could circulate round and around any sort of a serene and relaxed state that could turn out into a volatile and a tempestuous sphere that might be checked out into a static format of a morbid kind and then again could be versed out into a calm and a future harmonious stage once again over another bench upon another counter of a divers zone once more. All these trips could become possible by means of all types of nature forms of existing kinds that are currently staying 'alive'.

Knowledge about this systematic structure was gained and collected when the pensive nature and the physical forms had been sorted and diverted out from each other and therefore enabled us to 'screen and monitor' this existing sphere our from an 'isolated' and through a 'detached' phase. By means of this pause we had managed to stop the stereotyped effect that would always result out of nature forms and regulated them over our personal and pensive wishes and intents. This attitude had made us aware that existing and living were not the same.

Awareness that we are living and not existence was confirmed when wasting was avoided and a nature of investment had dawned upon us and motivated us to prepare for a future kind of a sphere that was recognized since we had distanced ourselves from the present state in order to think about future consequences. Hence a style, a fashion, a method, along with an infusion of existing kinds were reflected, applied, projected and inverted and were all delegated into modes of 'thoughts'.

Developing, production, converting and preparations were therefore designed in order to conduct existing forms and not the other way round.

Consequently nature forms were forked, formed, formatted into all sorts of images and hence manipulated in order to tender out more for the future that had been made clear and obvious by the past that was remembered and exploited through these intentions that brought awareness into 'us', about the differences of living and existing.

Whatever had ignited these initial sparks in order to be kindled out into our own minds cannot be included or validated out into these papers here since only existence is being defined and not 'living'.

Humanity had managed to be promoted and evolve into this existing sphere by means of essential kinds of information that had been relayed over from generations to others for no apparent reason, purpose or motives since the messengers or couriers were often unaware of the meanings of their contents. Although these kinds of messages were probable not even understood they were commonly relayed and transmitted from generation to generations either through traditions, folklore, saying or ritual in the manners of gestures, customs, adages or prayers, through occasions of joy, sorrow, pain or relief and consequently have ended up into our own laps right here and now.

These strange and enigmatic kind of messages holding the most amazing kinds of cryptic codes of messages in their emblematic forms of contents were strangely enough never discarded, dumped or just ignored which would have made the lives of these poor souls of messengers or prophets a lot more easier for them considering that they could never make head or tails what these sorts of 'mumbo jumbo' that they had been stuck and burdened with had contained in them. It is a mystery how and why these messages that had no apparent value had eventually ended up being forwarded and presented out to us.

These useless types of strange codes of information (some of which are going to be mentioned and cited into these papers here) had after all successfully managed to reach us just the same.

A universal plan seems to keep unfolding in order to present out some sort of assistance towards future generations that are always ahead of us.

A regular media for these sorts of messages are the various types of religious rituals that human nature had often performed all along through various different kinds of civilizations.

The fact that we might not approve or understand these kinds of activities does not necessary mean that these ceremonies do not have any valid aim, reason or intent in their crazy or weird acts that some of them might have.

These sorts of unfamiliar events could also be noticed to be happening even around us during these present times as well.

Most of us, who are grandparents might have

requested assistance from our grandchildren in order to give us some sort of advice so as to handle some sort of a digital device to which these young toddlers seems to have been well acquainted before they had been born. On the other hand most of us of a certain age might still have memories of the acrobatic feats that we used to perform which used to get us more in trouble than into hospitals because we had an urge to exercise our body more than our brains.

Nature seems to be preparing our children towards a digital kind of future age and had done its best in the past decades in order to build us towards a physical environment that was awaiting inside a factory for us to exercise what had been gained.

Our nature kind seems to walk astride with existing forms towards a future stage that is ready in store for us. Through this mode our physical abilities are being pedaled along our pensive thoughts that are revolving around existing forms that are being strained to present us more with the results that we would want in the future.

Thus we might state that we are currently 'screening, supervising, monitoring and sanctioning' all this kind of a sphere by our physical abilities and through our pensive conduct that enables us to manage and regulate whatever should happen next out of a selective conduct of a past existing tense.

By means of this detached attitude that could manipulate certain forms according to what we expect to get from them we had became the official administrators over this whole kind of a universe. All of this was possible because current affairs were being debated in an orderly manner, and the physical movements were being exercised over the limits that we had managed previously.

Existing barriers were currently opened and new domains were explored by means of ambition that was motivated and directions that were studied well beforehand.

All of these ambitions had been ingrained into us during a primitive age, but these sorts of missions had been officially determined out into a regulated system when 'democracy' had been fashioned out into a formal manner.

These events had all occurred in a systematic manner around 300 BC over in Athens.

The cradle of philosophy along with awareness of physical fitness are widely attributed to the Greek classical era that both were taking place circa 300 BC.

Epistemology seemed to have been cultured and flourished over there as it had never ever been done at anywhere else. Knowledge was discussed and debated over at that particular place in a manner that had never been made or managed out ever before. Great philosopher had emerged and a quest for knowledge had ensued with great minds that had contributed towards wisdom as has never ever been equaled as yet.

A great exponent upon this field was Socrates (469-399BC).

He had excelled so much in this field as to be decreed by the Greek gods to be 'the wisest man that had ever lived'. A form of an expression that is synonym with the character of this great man was when he had expressed those unforgettable words that 'he only knew that he knew nothing'. This simple phrase has been repeated out frequently ever since.

The tabular raza attitude or as it is most commonly known, in the academic field as a 'blank slate cleared from any previous cobwebs' mentality is regularly being advised to be adopted by new students who must make space in their brain to learn out a new subject. Teaching could only be learned through a conduct that is based upon a clear platform that must be uninhibited by other contents that would obstruct a new subject to be learnt.

This sort of an exercise suggests that the tools and instruments have got to be 'polished and cleaned' for another mission that could never be made possible if it has not a finite ambition laid out upon which it could flourish.

All the past forms of inclinations and orientations have got to be cleared out of the way in order to make more room for furniture in order to hold new looks for fresh items to be installed into our heads. The body and mind have got to be directed over a new sort of format, whilst the brain must have enough space in order to retain and hold a fresh attitude to accept inside them new 'thoughts'. A kind of an 'Academy' and a sort of an 'Arena' have got to be managed and directed by a syndicate that could govern and administer a system for the benefit of the establishment.

This was 'democracy' at its best since the 'establishments' and the 'senates' had successfully administered a nation for the benefit of the people with the mandate that was delegated out by the residents for a limited term.

A system that is based over these aspects have to rotate

over a pensive conduct and would need to be based over physical capabilities in order to be effectively employed and successfully performed.

This process had been performed by humanity when the physical and the pensive means had been stopped from rotating into aspects of cause and effect cycling without an aim and were concentrated and focused upon what was best and useful for 'us' to do.

The Greek 'democratic' system had been copied out from the human body and conducted upon a nation in a regulated institutional format.

The senate were delegated to administer the potentials of their citizens because they had been chosen for their integrity and leadership that they owned and possessed and positioned out as syndicates.

Over these same gradients and lines are the movements of the body when controlled by us to perform whatever we might decide to do.

These very same potentials were initially used and utilized out by 'Homo Sapience' who had gained the merits of a 'man who knows' by these abilities that were being steered by what this creature wanted to compose.

This was the 'secret formula' that had made the Greek nation the center of civilization and had also been the method that 'Homo Sapience' had been strained out from other primates and effectively our kinds had also came out.

The period when the Greek nations had reached the peak of a democratic state was when the 'academy' and the 'arena' were being managed and directed by the senate in a detached manner that was isolated from both these sorts of establishments.

Epistemology and physical fitness were being exercised, practiced, tested and contested into two separate and divers fields that were left to be administrated by the organizers that were experts and professionals over their respective spheres. Consequently an arena that concentrated upon physical fitness was being encouraged and recognized for the standards achieved by means of discipline over the body, and intellectuals were being respected for delivering clever thoughts that had been debated at the forum to be utilized by the state.

More information was being given out to the citizen and stronger soldiers were being disciplined out even more.

Both these establishments grew, developed, matured and became distinguished for their great works and achievements because the 'governing bodies' revered and respected their 'nature forms' and avoided to interfere or intervene into their respective fields since their aims and targets were directed and aimed at the benefits of the state to be enjoyed by the citizens of that nation.

The present kinds of Olympic games that are still being held worldwide are a reminder of those days gone bye.

Harnessing, controlling and managing the conditions of the physical abilities of the body are the optimum targets that are aimed during these forms of exhibitions. Whilst on the other hand epistemology was also born during this period when philosophers were also busy tackling out issues that were most important towards society. A 'democratic' state that was staged, directed and managed in accordance to current sorts of necessities was being rolled, evolved, tackled and steered towards what was best for the state and the citizens.

Although both these enterprises were independent over their own administrative roles their finite aims and objectives were always towards promoting and evolving more the state and the citizens. On the other hand the 'state and the people' always paid due respect and reverence to both of them in return. The esteem that was versed out towards the philosophers was because they educated the people more whilst the respect for the athletes was because they were presenting out more security and protection towards the state. These kinds of ideals may still be above our present forms of standards because we still tend to 'stone the messenger' and 'idolize our computers' rather than toil and nurture more our own heritage and appreciate better our own roots by educating and cultivating what we have for our own sake rather than to brag about what we don't have or own.

During those past days the Geek nations gave us the best sorts of examples of how to be de-marked and be organized in order to decide and conduct over what is important and essential without being restrained into a stereotype style of a cause and effect fashion that would render us sterile and impotent if ever we get caught inside such an existing morbid frame of a cyclic trend.

By means of exercising the physical abilities at the Olympics games and through the various forms of intellectual debates that they were regularly conducting the Greek nations had considered themselves to be more civilized than their neighbors whom they regarded out as being 'barbarians' because they had no class.

Their neighbors who lacked over and upon these

qualities and abilities were deemed to be 'savages' just because their personal control was lacking and they never cared to be better informed and consequently they were easily snared whenever they were coaxed inside any kind of a trap. This progressive attitude had been gained by means of controlling the vibes of the sensual body towards effective movements and by treating mental issues before they happen to occur in order to be well prepared for any sort of a casual existing event.

The Greek nation had successfully managed to direct and control a 'body and mind' through an 'entity' that governed without being 'influenced' or 'inclined' in a strict mode towards a targeted defined end.

At the philosophical academy precious kinds of virtues were being appreciated for social reasons, whilst at the gymnasium physical talents were regarded as essentials in order to safeguard their various sorts of enterprises. A cause and effect process was controlled and managed by deviating and managing it over its own kinds of merits that was revolving over its own priorities of credits by restraining and harnessing sensual passion.

Two autonomous and separate bodies of two different skills and abilities had been appreciated for their existing roles by the authorities of ancient Greece who had a senate that was controlling and supervising all of this in a detached and isolated manner above and aloft from them both.

What 'Homo Sapience' had managed to conduct over existing forms, the Greek nations had utilized over their state and later on the Roman senates exploited it in order to occupy the known world of those days. The secret weapon that was behind the Roman Empire was contained in the mode of discipline and organization that their legionnaires practiced and employed over the battlefields. These professional soldiers exploited out their own potentials by taking advantage over the conduct of their opponents who used to be driven into chaos since they lacked organization and discipline that was the secret weapon of the professional Roman soldiers.

The Roman generals were most successful due to the orderly manner and skillful discipline that they used to practice and exercise in physical and in the pensive fields which they were promoting and monitoring regularly and so they ended up being experts over these qualities. Strategic formations over strong positions used to be manipulated and exploited by the soldiers and generals who were expert at this game of chess but were not the owner of this 'board'. Over these kinds of principles a nation 'enthroned an emperor' and upon this conduct the citizens of Rome were feared and respected all over the world in those days.

These kinds of historical details might soon be forgotten and erased out from our minds. This is because that since these events could not present or furnish us with a new outlet from which we could develop something else we tend to discard all this sort of useless information away from us. This is a natural cycle of life that has to spiral over and away rather than keep on circulate round in an innuendo form that is bound to get us nowhere if it has no aim in the terminal end.

We had experienced various episodes when an invention had lost the genes of its own heritage.

One clear example is the mode of how our various

forms of languages had all evolved into these present sorts of colloquial conversations that we are able to hold between us and none of us seems to know from whence all these gestures had arrived or begun. Another case in point is how we had managed to compute the imaged form of the 'zero' that is in itself the biggest kind of a paradox if one has to think and ponder over its contents.

Ironically we tend to compose so many adages and proverbs that all connects us with our past but the mother of these sorts of paradoxes that must be awarded toward the imaged form of the 'zero' has never been made up yet to remind us of this dark and empty sphere. Surely it is the most hilarious, funny, entertaining joke that anyone could make out from this empty space that is bound to interest and fill us all with gust of laughter at no expense at all if it has to be explained in full. This is most understandable because no one would want to keep on ranting over a cyclic kind of a repetitive role that could never be awarded out any sort of merit since this form is void and empty of any sorts of credits.

Our current kinds of needs directs us in order to concentrate over a specific future topic that sometimes alienates us away from the very reason why we had initially followed along these sorts of lines of logics.

For example some of us might even have forgotten that in the olden days distances used to be calculated out into the numbers of paces made in order to reach a destination which later on they were named out as 'feet' and are currently being deleted out into a metric system that would eventually erase the origin that had been developed out of our own kinds of personal organs. We are currently being more precise and have to define better our conduct and performances in a more exact manner and might need to meter these gauged amount even better still than these present ones. The needs for existence inhibits us with an attitude that would not allow us in order to look back at useless nature forms that could not be milked out anymore. The origins of these modes would eventually be buried, discarded, dumped or disposed from our recollections because we could never extract out anything from these versions that have become obsolete since our current needs do not match them anymore.

Our own personal version that sustain and supports us are all contained into our pensive and physical sphere. A brief description of these two vital and important 'nature forms' might explain out better our physical academy and pensive arena that we all have and possess.

The physical kinds of exercises that we currently perform in order to keep us all active and fit are conducted out through the sensual movements of 'vision, audition, feeling and digestion'.

A two way kind of a system manages the directions of these pulses and impulses that we tend to regulate and also command towards a better grade that is also being defined out by us.

These sorts of physical pulses are regularly being felt, indulged to some kind of an extent of a degree until over indulged, regretted and would be regressed and reversed to be corrected, refined and adjusted in order to try and satisfy 'us' towards a better merited grade at an extreme end.

The graphic image of this arena takes the form of a zigzagging path that could alter and be changed whenever it needs to be charged and extended out further more again and would be steered upwards if it has to achieve a higher gradient along a next phase.

All of these sorts of physical movements could be imaged by various forms of modes of vibes of 'pulling and pushing', 'waving and vibrating', butting and rubbing', as well as 'picking and tickling' in order to elicit out a 'pixel' that would be transferred over towards our pensive 'board'.

This deciding 'board' is also 'us' that could de-mark these imaged conducts into formats after they had been computed out by our pensive minds. This spiraling process is known as perceptions after modes are conceived.

This form of an inspirational attitude is conducted over a pensive sphere that has to pivot over the axle of a physical frame whenever it is being exercised or activated out by us.

This operation could rotate out at any sort of speed that might make us go dizzy or keep us glazed against an image that our nature forms could not keep up or along those current forms of spatial types of experiences.

All these pensive modes are contained into the aspects of intentional images of 'reflection, projection, application and also inverting' about which we become ultra-conscious about these wares that would be turned around into 'forms of thoughts' for 'us'.

Thus conceptions over perceptions are handled, managed, directed and organized out by 'us' who govern our own aspects of 'existence' towards our benefits that are all being utilized in order to support our own 'lives' we have.

The central aspect at the 'heart' of this pensive frame is carried out by means of an organ known as the 'thalamus'.

This organic pensive form confers with the physical throbbing of the heart that we have pounding into our chest with the difference that it rotates in order to relay the pulses that would need to be framed out for us instead of being pumped.

This form of a membrane is conducting our brain by means of a cerebral cortex instead of valves. One is beating around some form of concepts, whilst the other is busy presenting out what had been achieved in a similar manner that 'democracy' is governed, run, managed and directed out by means of the citizens in society.

The very same principle of a 'democratic' system that had been flashed out by the Greek nations had also been infused inside the human nature stature long before it had been officially applied to govern out a country in the same fashioned that our kind of an 'existing' body is managed by our 'lives'.

When humanity was conducting out this system our genetic strain had been defined out as having reached out the level of awareness regarding existing forms and our instincts and sentiments were being controlled into the imaged frame of 'thoughts' regulated out exclusively by our 'lives' and not by 'cause and effect'.

Nature forms were being recognized and organized by means of information that was currently being collected out instinctively and passionately that deviated out our lives from static and morbid forms.

Experiences was maturing and cultivating physical

abilities in order to be performed in an expert manner whilst retaliation over the least provocation was being regulated in a disciplined way so as to be vented out when the time was ripe.

The human body was conducting out physical activities in an organized manner over what was being decided out to be best which was not necessary always most convenient for us.

When we had evolved to this stage the body and mind were being directed in a democratic style that was later on, copied out into a formal manner in an institutional mode by the people of Greece in exactly the same way.

All of this had been achieved since our lives had managed to stay detached and isolated from a cause and effect existing cord that was altered and changed by means of our administrative abilities that were disciplined and informed to be harnessed and controlled and not respond towards existing modes of 'cause and effect'.

Humanity had universally managed to collect information out from existing kinds and utilized their resources to be exercised in order to promote and cultivate lives without being swept and swamped along the ripples of nature forms since we became aware by taking note of whatever is going on.

This operation was able to give humanity an advantage that was based upon an edge of a physical nature kind that hinged upon a pensive ledge that is now commonly being referred by us as, 'know ledge'. These conditions enabled the image of a 'Homo Sapience' in order to develop out into a creature that 'knew some forms of the nature of knowledge' as well as 'being aware about this existing sphere' through an academy that was currently giving out lectures in a common language of a 'cause and effect' that evolved into perceptions and conceptions instead.

This system was copied out exactly by the Greek nations when the Olympics and the Academy were in vogue during their glorious heydays when duties and responsibilities were currently being regarded and acknowledged for their own merits of importance that they contained or performed for the benefit of the state. It was most natural that when any kind of a creature would have learned to control and manipulate existence they would become most grateful towards existing forms.

This must have been the reason that had steered humanity to conduct rituals, magic, praying and sacrifices that nowadays do not have any more meaning to us.

These sorts of drills had been performed because forms of nature were being appreciated very much and so they were being regarded out to be 'gods' to them.

Primitive cultures and ancient forms of societies are renowned to conduct out various norms of rituals and taboos that we might not be able to understand. We have not been the first to regard these kinds of ceremonies as a lot of nonsense and a waste of time during these forms of lessons because mavericks, truants and rascals who never liked 'history lessons' must have been over there as well.

Conducting a form of a 'tabula rasa' over any sort of an establishment is a hard and difficult kind of a task to be accomplished out by anyone. This painful process of having to change or delete former kind of customized attitudes into the bony brains of those sorts of primitive beings must have been a difficult task for any teacher or tutor during those days as it is during these times over here in the same way as well.

During those dark ages when survival had centered over greed and the nature of security was focused over and upon necessities, the culture of education formed upon strict discipline must have been a luxury that was even difficult to the elite let alone to the common citizen. Being burdened by their daily turmoil's, when their kinds of objectives must have been hunting, trapping, farming, hoarding and fleeing from all sorts of danger and hazard, the nature of existing was a most formidable kind of a task for anyone in those days. In an untamed kind of a world surrounded by all sorts of animals, beasts and noisy neighbors who could digest anything without using any sorts of forks or spoons, it must have been more than a mouthful for humanity in order to compose a pensive aspect that could be able to concentrate over living when existing had been the order on the agenda of those day. Trying to compute out any sort of knowledge out from that sphere must have been an impossible task for any primitive creature to be able to exercise or compose during those heydays. In spite of all these kinds of tempestuous conditions humanity did managed to conceive an operation that enabled a race to be 'strained' out of that trend and was able to supervise and scrutinize all that was going on around them and therefore had became aware and recognized out 'living' that had consequently surfaced out from a frame of existing.

Out from an existing state when beds had never been issued with any sorts of linen sheets and bedtime had never been set out yet, a kind of a being must have came out with a ' frame of devices' that were promoted out from 'cause and effect' into a democratic system, that was later on copied in the same style by the Greek nations in an institutional way through the senate that had government them out so well. These major reforms had enabled a kind of a personality in order to be restrained form reacting over the slightest mistake and to take precautions that in the future these barriers would be considered as a challenge rather than as a deterrent and could be contested if well armed and well composed beforehand.

An inborn academy of study was conceiving new ideas inside the 'temple' of humanity that had to make room for an 'arena' to concentrate out more samples of these existing forms into the body of a better developed kind of a new race that was aware of living due to this new ambient that was consequently taking formation. A cyclic effect that was halted and sometimes paused was assessed, graded and stored towards knowledge or wisdom for future references to be tested or performed towards similar cases that were consequently being assured even more of success.

Imaged kind of information were being gathered at the expense of experience that were being noted over nature forms after having been used and utilized either by brain or by brawn towards new sorts of challenges whenever another similar need arose. A primitive sort of an 'Academy' along with a 'Gymnasium' of an ancient formation had been used to promote and evolve a creature to gain knowledge from these existing experiences to administer out lives better still.

An organic system that had been based over a democratic principles had enabled a form of a being in order evolve out of existing modes and be promoted out from a primitive ambient that had been rotating over a cause and effect stationary and stagnated existing phase. This prehistoric kind of a process had been made and maintained well before the ancient people of Greece had managed to civilize their nation into the kind of an establishment of a democratic nation that had amazed the ancient world. Humanity had managed to achieve this high grade during the times when 'homo sapience' was still running around bare footed, unshaven, and might have only managed to get hold of just a thong in order to cover all that he possessed over this earth.

Out from a chaotic period when existence presented out regular challenges towards lives, a pensive conduct had been given out space to think, and physical strength was being reserved in a disciplined manner in order to be used and utilized towards vital and important kinds of issues that enabled this creature to come out on top and in front of all these kinds of existing modes of cyclic trends.

Homosapiens did manage to 'transforms nature forms into information' in order to use it as a sort of an 'edge to be gathered into knowledge' that were consequently transferred into 'gods and idols' that might be defined out as 'talent and virtues' by us in our time.

Living and existing had to rotate and revolve over and upon these terminal forms towards a useful cause that had to be decided and sanctioned out by our 'us' in the end. This circular aspect over a rotary mode had been the form of inspiration that was grasped in order to evolve and be promoted out from all these sorts of existing kinds of nature forms and would consequently be lodged into an amount of graded form of 'intelligence'.

During this process there were various occasions when ambitious persons found this process to have stagnated over vane cause and these rotary aspects were presenting out mundane results of an innuendo kind of a style ending up into some style of a cul-de-sac.

A very special person who wanted to make us aware of these sorts of inhibitions and conditions that would reverse our nature kinds into a stereotype frame once again was a Greek philosopher by the name of Plato who had lived around 427 – 347 BC.

He must have noted a cyclic innuendo style regulating out our lives out of which we could never be able to develop anything new for as long as we would keep rotating around our 'current needs and demands' that he must have portrayed them out as existing 'cause and effects'.

He had very cleverly portrayed this 'robotic' nature of a 'zombie' style when he described out our nature kinds 'chasing images and shadows inside a subterranean dark cave'.

Both these aspects could enable us to understand out better a stereotype imaged of a character that is inhibited by sets of conditions that are blindly followed and accepted which effectively would impede out any sort of progress to be made.

This elite fashion of a paragon in the manner of a modern Phoenix which must have been wished to come out of this subterranean cave has not evolved out yet even though the burning flame of the Olympiads had crossed the world over and the Academy of statistic are now being handled out by means of computers instead of our organic brains. Our human existing kinds are still regulated out by inhibitions and conditionings to these present times as well.

Now that the introductory stage had been composed the next chapter is meant in order to define out what 'nature forms' of existence actually means to us.

Over the same lines that had now been grooved out would this symposium commence and be constructed in order to support what had been introduced out briefly.

These papers are intended in order to examine out this existing sphere from within the contents of our own sorts of lives that we all have and possess.

This sort of an Odyssey might even go further and could also target out some 'establishments' that are imbedded into a morbid role over which no substance could ever come out for as long as they do not make an effort and get out of that hole into which they might have got now stuck.

This gauntlet that is being slapped across the board could now be dispensed or disposed depending whether if the 'gods' are steering them or if they are being motivated by their own shadow that could only be seen in the daytime.

This diagonal process that is being expressed through this introductory stage is an analogue style over which this dissertation has to be based that is about to describe existence by means of the organisms of our own lives that we have.

A final word of thanks and gratitude have to be awarded out to the society of the 'museum of heritage' by whose courtesy and diligent manners these kinds precious gems have now ended up into the palms of our hands.

And should ever the question of whether 'to be or not to be' would be doubted out again, then the answer would always surf up if we log over the slogan of

'Verbum Carum Factum Est'.

HOMO SAPIENS

Why am I here! ?
What makes me tick?
Is it the food or just the medicine!
Who am I in this strange place?
Is this the self, with just a face!
Is this a dream or just a scheme?
Played out by someone who is called out 'me'!
I get confused within my own self
I am the master as well as the slave
Existing in substance that always change
Structured by bones and wrinkled by age.
Residing around this quadrant frame
Bundled around inside a name.
All these factors are known as facts.
Yet no facts could come out exact.
The pensive steers around the physique
Instructed out by my own technique
Surely this cube could be defined
If a state of living into it is confined.
Even old Plato had tried to explain
That our scurrying is made in vain,
Chasing around images and shadows
Around these subterranean burrows.
But a light had been shed bigger than a sun
Through the mystic phrase of the 'Yahweh'
By which Living address this frame.

Wisdom was filled with intelligence
Which is a case unknown to us,
'HOMOSAPIENSE'

THE FORMULA THAT TREATS 'EXISTING'

The nature forms of existence were all created from an outside zone.

This current sphere had been staged over a rotary frame.

These logistics and statistics have no former or previous kinds of logarithms inserted into their fashioned styles.

Thus existence cannot ever be versed out philosophically but has to be termed out grammatically and recognized by our means of abilities that we have and possess.

This stated version is not to be considered as another kind of an invention but as a symbolic image that existence had been formed and made out by a Creator. Therefore these kinds of testimonials have got to be presented out from us but would need and require some sort of evidence in order to confirm that this version is based over and upon a stable frame.

Our own kinds of lives are all witnessing occurrences and happenings inside this sphere but a form of an alibi should be brought forth in order to confirm this formula as being seen through a periscope that is not immersed into this spherical kind of a zone down here.

Over this legitimate aspect has to be expected a conclusive result that is going to be extracted out from 'us' and consequently it would be supported by an independent 'alibi' that would be forwarded in the manner of a proxy out at the end.

Hence if all these statements would all be 'balanced, matched, equated and twinned' up with our own kinds of 'selves' then by means of the method of counter and cross references this sort of a theory should deserve to be considered out to be as reliable as 'us'.

This sort of a process might be regarded out to be some sort of a scheduled program that is being based over the echoes of the ripples that had been recorded out from a gap that had been made out by this kind of a universe. Considering that our versions could only survive over a cyclic frame that is currently spiraling around this sphere, therefore validating out an existing function could only be made over whatever is being staged and performed around here. Thus we have to note out this current existing system and relate it with us in order to define it out in context with the sorts of lives that we have and posses.

Through this consternating aspect we could be able to investigate out creation over it axles that are rotating upon a version that is identical to our pensive and physical abilities out of which our lives could comprehend and understand all that is happening and evolving around this sphere. So by means of delegating out our abilities in order to be organized into an embalmed corpse contained into forms of statistics we could be able to confirm out logical conclusions that would have been styled and fashioned upon living over existing factions.

Over this synthetic kind of a benchmark we could plan out our intentions that we have and upon this mission we could embark in order to understand a version that is organized out in a similar manner exactly just like us.

Along this organic trail we could be able to define out existence and upon our version we could be able to compose modes that would relate outwards what had been registered from feedbacks contained inside their types of membranes.

Therefore this cyclic trend could initiate over our own sorts of ingredients in order to describe what is around all of us.

These sorts of logarithms could all be defined out by means of our own recognition when scrolled this way:

- An entity would note.
- A person would contest.
- A being is in context.
- A self is established.

Out from these aspects of our lives we could zoom them out again backwards and gauge our images once again.

The results would all surf up into these versions as listed down here:

- An equated sphere would verse out an entity.
- Any matched couple would verse out a person.
- A universal phase would verse out a being.
- A deleted byte would verse out a self.

All of these versions that had been derived out from various sorts of zones could now be contrasted against each other in order to stage them out separately over different lineage of strata in order to verify this existing method once more, this way:

- A relaxed habitat would verse out a serene state.
- A tranquil habitat would verse out a calm state.
- A static habitat would verse out a morbid state.
- A tempestuous habitat would verse out a violent state.

Once again out from these data, details, aspects and symbols of those previous synthetic structured designs a revision could be staged out in order to confirm what had been vented out from us, once again:

- An 'entity' is always styled out of a 'pole' position of our live.
- A 'person' is always staged out of 'matter' formation into our lives.
- A 'being' is always infused out from 'time and space' into our lives.
- A 'self' is always a token of reference in 'relation' to our sorts of lives.

Therefore since our lives had been 'styled, staged, established and fashioned' out from the contents of these ingredients, then existence of our lives is earmarked under the cover of these factors that would always be linked along with them all.

Out from under the cloaks of our current frames of lives we could therefore sketch out a synchronized content of effigies that sustain and supports us over these kinds of ranks that our lives must always have;-

A. Time/space.
B. Relativity.
C. Polarity.
D. Matter.

This whole structure could be deciphered once again and be 'conducted, managed, focused and treated' by us in order to extract out an explanation as could be shown over here:

(a) Contained into ' kinds, sorts, logics and statistics'
(b) Modeled over 'codes, grades, features and characteristics'
(c) Fashioned upon 'time, space, records and experiences'.
(d) Noted around 'types, style, genes and forms'.

All of these zones, spheres, phases and grades could again be reviewed out and manoeuvred again backwards towards where they had all originally came out from in order to confirm that this kind of a treaty is correct and precise.

By means of these frames of counter references then statistics could be scrutinized out from their styles of cross sections through the amounts of ingredients being noted inside their forms.

Hence these existing kinds of nature forms could all be 'equated, balanced, matched and twinned' over again in order to confirm what had been described out from our own sorts of lives as well. Therefore by means of comparing out the nature form against our lives all the factors of existence could again be logged out forth once more from out of us once more.

This analogue manner of a synthetic style could again be raked out forward once more in order to present the seeds that have nurtured us to evolve over here:

- A 'being' consist of existence over 'time and space' tenure.
- An 'entity' is a form that exists in 'relation' towards this sphere.
- A 'self' consists of pixels and bytes having a 'pole' positioned of existence over here.
- A 'person' is a 'matter' form that could conceive existing knowledge out from this current stage.

This complex system could again be changed and altered out from its present state and could be fashioned out into a more advanced style that is beyond our present existing types of lives we now have.

An elevated imaged version of our own kinds of lives could also be defined out through this current system into which we now all exists but could not convey out any sort of meaning from their spiked style which are more in the future than we presently are.

These shadowed future versions of our lives are all contained into the aspects of 'souls, essence, ghosts and spirits' about which we might be conversant but we are only acquainted with just their spectrums.

Although by now it might have been made clear that existence is paved and lined out into a cube, but our own kinds of lives could only be imaged in the form of a tripod and could only be diagnosed through a style of a hexagon.

These anomalies could also be explained along the structure of this claimed theory as well for as long as those images are being made out from 'us' these contents have features and imagination composed and deducted out by 'us' in order to note our kind or to denote what we have.

Therefore we always tend to describe the framework of the existence of our lives by means of one of 'us' and so we might mistakenly conclude that our system is composed by just three in all, or else we might note all our version by modes of deduction and include our inspecting mode twice which would result in five and not four.

Hence we could all image our current lives to be constructed into the mode of a pyramid that is supported over a quadrant existing frame.

Only our own kind of a Creator has and owns a perfect model of an equated type of a Trinity since no kind of an existing platform could be found to support Him.

Our own personal kinds of physical and pensive nature forms keep on protracting out into existing frames that would all keep their quadrant style all the way.

Our physical conditions that we have could be noted out from the senses of 'seeing, hearing, feeling and smelling/digesting' that we possess.

These kinds of nature forms would always become information when they are turned out into thought by means of our own sort of pensive conduct.

This computing operation would 'reflect, project, apply and invert' sensual pulses and present them out over into formatted types of thoughts.

This whole operation could only be possible managed and directed out by us for as long as existence is being synchronized in the manner of – matter, time/space, relativity and polarity that supports and assist us all to live.

All these details might not be approved since our view of an existing ambient might not be synchronized but focused upon a particular aspect that interest us more than the rest.

Therefore a second opinion out from an arbiter should resolve this case in a definite mode if it is being presented out from an 'outsider' who is not a resident into this existing sphere.

Only our Mentor who is not 'enclosed' inside these defined parameters is able and capable to state out any sort of a voiced proxy regarding this existing sphere since He is everywhere and His words should prove the best alibi of substance to support what had been said.

Confirmation regarding this case was proclaimed out when our Mentor voiced out His relationship towards us to be known and recognized into the contents of the word of 'Yahweh' and ever since then, this kind of a phrase had been considered out to be the axioms of the logarithms upon which this existing system oscillates and the contents of those words were framed out as the slogan that signifies out from where we had all came out from.

This solemn declaration that had been given over to us is cited out through the Bible along the lines of the Exodus in chapter 3, and is still considered to be holy and sacred even during these present times as well.

On this memorable occasion when Moses had met

God 'face to face' he had asked Him to be contained and enveloped up into some kind of a name by which we could summon and call Him out over here whenever we want to invite and beckon Him to come around into this existing kind of a universe.

An answer that rotated over a pun and contained into an opaque nature was most suited to be given out for us in order to ponder and compare this system of a cyclic frame with our types of lives that we presently have and possess. This imaged bridge between existing forms and our lives had been aligned together by means of a cord that is not curled around like this universe and on the other hand does not depend upon previous nature kind in order to define what is currently being said to support the genes of those words.

That particular reply had been addressed and given out from the font of the Author and Mentor Himself.

Thus the style of the answer that had been conveyed to us does not require a cursor in order to assists those letters to go along with our line of thinking because they hold thoughts to be wound around them instead.

The version that was given out does not have to rely over or upon a priori in order to be acknowledged because it is locked and lodged over its own kind of phrase.

This phrase is not to be considered the profile of the Administrator but a portfolio of the mystery of existence that is versed out by means of the codes that regulates us in order to acknowledge the legitimate proprietor of this whole universe.

Therefore since existence oscillates and revolves around and about this universe in a similar manner just like those words we could only understand them and could never bend or twist them to convey a different message instead.

Thus inside that expression is contained and enclosed all the objects and subjects of nature forms that are needed and required to inform us about this whole kind of a universe.

Although what had been versed out could never have meant out anything to the people of those days yet this version had been relayed over to us inside a sacred 'baton' and now has successfully ended up into the palms of our hands.

Their sense of intuition must have made them aware that those words would be most important at a future stage and so they had done their very utmost in order to preserve them in their original state over which those words had initially been proclaimed.

The memorable answer that had been given out is contained into the four words of 'Yod, He, Vay and He' and when transliterated consonantally they are denoted as 'Y H V H'.

Ever since that time even these four letters had been enveloped into a safekeeping casing of an 'Adonai' being addressed to them so as to protect them from being expressed out into vulgar modes that might blunt out the sacred textured frame into which they had been versed out in the first place. Not only that, but even their formatted style had been wrapped up into an enigmatic content of a 'password' in order to protect the fashioned type of grammar so as to hold and keep them intact as well. Hence these four letter words were being referred to as the 'Tetragrammaton' in order to protect them from being profaned in any sort of an imaginable kind of a way.

This kind of a sacred pun that had been given out to us contains the formatted words inside its own version that pronounces the theory of our existence as presented out from the undisputed Authority of this whole creation.

All the logarithms of this whole kind of a universe are contained and enclosed into the format model of that sacred phrase.

When those words had been pronounce out, all of existence was brought out into a standstill in the manner that a soldier or a private would freeze to attention whenever they are being addressed out by the High Command.

In an albeit moment in time the ligaments of this universe had stood still in order to receive fresh vitamins being injected into them so as to continue the mission over the contents of those words. Out from this focal aspect we could inspect our cyclic trend and by concentrating over that version we could confirm that sustainable and stability are currently rotating and revolving just like that framed phrased version which had been given to us.

Out from the trademark of the style of those words we could grade out our own level of intelligence and over that slogan we could frame out the features of all this kinds of an existing sort of a universe.

After all this time the word of 'Yahweh' had again been presented out in order to vouch that this universe had been created out from a synchronized source out from which all existing forms had originally been created out from.

Through this panoramic and spectacular scene space travel would seem to be mediocre and the intelligence of science would all look crude when compared towards what is contained into that phrase.

The version of those four letter words have given us more meaning about this existing kind of a universe than all those capsules that had been sent out in order to investigate what had already been confirmed out through the Bible a long time ago. Existence is still being held mummified into those words that are still wound and curled around their own tendered frame which have not extinguished or had ever been proved out wrong as yet.

The ingredients contained into those words confirms that our lives are not meant to remain indefinitely and eternally inside this four dimensional sphere over here. Through the modes of the style of those words all the information that is needed about our existence had been presented and forwarded out to us in order to confirm that our kinds would eventually spiral out from this kind of a cyclic frame of a universe.

That phrase could be imaged out as some sort of a capsule that orbits over its own axles and consternates around its belt in a similar manner just like our own kind of a universe that is currently spiraling around an unknown item that has never been revealed or discovered out as yet.

This finite or terminal spot over which we direct and steer our nature forms could only be recognized out through the model image form of a Trinity as otherwise our version would keep on spiraling around in circles in a similar manner as this universe is trailing towards an unspecified aim at the very end.

Modern kinds of technology cannot ever be able to extract any new devices out of the sacred phrase of 'Y H VH' since those holy words had been composed out by the Author and further computation over this version could not furnish or supply us with more information than we could possible load up our mortal minds.

Only through respect and reverence could these sacred words be utilized in order to help our version so as to evolve into a higher graded rated sphere than we are currently and presently being staged upon right now.

Our present existing version had been addressed out from a station that is stable and fixed although our own personal kinds of impressions makes us all believe that we are straight and everything else is crooked and bent around our linear kinds of lives. The contents of those words had made it clear and obvious that the nature forms of existence are all synchronized over a cyclic aspect that could be imaged out from the version of that phrase that had been presented out over to us.

The Latin dictum that had been ranted out by the Christian church since medieval times and is contained into the words of 'Verbum Carum Factum Est' could have been derived and copied out of the version of the Tetragrammaton.

The original version of 'Yod He Vay He' is presently better known now as 'Yahweh', whilst even this word is currently being colloquially pronounced out as 'Jehovah' instead, due to our form of dialect.

This word actually and literally means a 'witness' by its own kind of a defined mode of a design. Therefore by the support of this alibi that had been cited out to vouch for us, we can now conclusively state out that the factors of existence are all synchronized over this cyclic atmosphere of;-

'Time/space, matter, relativity and polarity' as had been confirmed out by the only suited kind of Authority over this subject that is outside these parameters of this entire frame of an establishment.

Over this current version our lives are being 'generated, engineered, geared and guaranteed' so as to live and exist forevermore for as long as we have faith upon and over the Original version contained into that 'hallow phrase' which were directly presented out to us by the Creator Himself.

WHERE HAVE WE COME FROM?

Searching and tracing our own sort of origin is a fundamental quest that humanity has always tried to discover.

Investigating our 'origin' and 'creation' would not be complete if either the 'being', 'self', 'entity' or our type of ''personalities' would be left out of this process.

This 'case' cannot leave out any angle unaccounted out of the 'framed' theory that had been presented out in these papers.

These verses must adhere, follow, support and sustain what had been previously been defined out.

Once again a rotary process of a cyclic trend would have to be intersected at various stages, in order to belt together life experience along with existing details in order to reach a common version that is acceptable on all front.

Over this platform has to be based imaged kinds of information that are related towards the objective of this current subject that is about to be undertaken.

By means of the physical abilities and pensive capacities this process should present out sane concepts for as long as they are 'balanced, equated, level and matched' with our kind of body and frame of mind that binds together existence with our style of lives.

We are all aware of our sensual conscious by means of the four senses of 'audition, digesting, sight and feeling' that we normally exercise physically.

We manage these modes through an intentional framework of 'reflection, application, projection and inverting' that we are ultra-conscious aware of as well. Our own kind of 'physical' origin had been handled and tackled in a professional manner by Darwin, a respected and eminent scientist as well as an anthropologist who lived more than 150 years ago.

His works was consequently published out and defined out into a book called 'On the origin of the species'. It had caused quite a stir, and even up to these days some prominent and influential characters are doing their utmost in order to discredit what is actually happening and occurring all around us regularly.

This kind of bedlam came about because the Christian church was concentrating over what has been written inside the scripture that never suggests that our ancestors had ever been the 'apes'. What had been presented out by Darwin's theory was thus seen as a challenge towards the literature contained inside the Holy Bible.

This historical conflict could have been avoided if our 'nature forms' were regarded out as 'existing' and 'living' separately.

Our kinds of genes had been created and versed out in order to evolve and be transformed towards another sphere from which we had been 'formed' and as well as 'made'.

Over these conditions we could inspect and speculate our origin and heritage that have to 'start' and 'initiate' from an organic structure as well as from a venue of creation that both have awarded us with noble qualities of 'living' and 'existing'.

We are currently being strained out and by means of an existing phase and consequently we all hope to return back to where we had originally been made as well.

Darwin had tried to tackle the quest of origin from the genealogical aspect without involving the font of creation, whilst the Christian church relied upon a model version of creation without taking into account the heritage of our forms of genetics models.

This research could have been more successful if existing conditions would have been investigated and an aspect of living would be accepted along every discovery being made.

This process had to be operated over two sides that had to treat our 'nature forms' out together since 'existing' and 'living' has to go hand in hand.

It is amazing how the Christian church had managed to overlook this 'crucial' aspect that our existing nature forms are to be recycled whilst the contents of our lives are to be retained and kept by us.

Sacred teachings had been transformed into academic form of meaningless sort of detailed kind of information. The very same teachings that was being preached, hammered and imprinted upon all its followers for thousands of years as a sort of a 'mission statement' was not being comprehended and understood at all because it failed to consider the 'verb' of the sentences that was being expressed and formed. For it had all been clearly explained in a very simple way that man had been 'formed' and 'molded' into a being of an 'entity, person and a self' just like our Mentor of one God in 'Three different kind of Personalities'. The Holy Bible seems to be able to reveal all of this basic and precious kind of information from which we can learn a lot and perhaps preach so very little.

In order to understand better this version and extract out an explanation from both ends we have to scrutinize better what the Bible has to say and keep in mind whatever Darwin had tried to define out as well.

Thus we have to note information out from the Holy scripture regarding creation, and also study whatever Darwin had found about our current form of surviving.

Darwin had based his theory over our kind of a person, whilst the Bible referred about human kind of creation sort.

Overlooking and disregarding all of this 'kind' of information could have been the reason why the Christian church had objected and rejected the theory that was presented out by Darwin regarded the nature of our 'line' of origin that could have given the impression that Mr. Adam was some form of an Ape.

It must have been most distressing to accept the fact that our own father smelt so much, was so bad looking and did not even have the decency to wear a leaf!

Although the Christian church could be held guilty of not accepting the theory of evolution it was also due to this obstinate attitude that the mystery of the Holy Trinity had managed to reach us to these present days.

The Christian church had always persisted in a most courageous manner that our Mentor of a singular kind of a God possess three different kind of nature of personalities that are independent and distinctively different as well as autonomous in their infinite power and potentials, which must not be considered or decreed as three different kinds of separate sort of divers sorts of gods.

This proclamation had presented our present civilization with the greatest form of a contradiction contained in a classical paradox that had never been equaled out as yet. No form of an organization or society worth its salt could have kept on existing after presenting out a paradox that could not even be understood by its own followers and members let alone by the outsiders of unbelievers.

Most miraculously the Christian church in a most amazing manner did manage to survive such a dreadful kind of a test in a most convincing manner, and what's more it was achieved with full flying kind of colors as well!

The Christian church was never able to explain in a logical manner the mystery of the 'Holy Trinity'.

Since no clear form of any sort of an explanation could ever be found or contrived in order to explain this puzzling form of a concept it was therefore concluded to be considered as a form of a 'Theological Mystery that would rests upon Faith'. This decision must have led many of her followers to go astray and away or perhaps they must have opted out from it, whilst other religions must certainly have ridiculed this form of a rigged type of a statement.

Many great thinkers were assigned in order to explain and reveal such a Mystery but no success was ever made upon this topic. Even the church most wise, thinker and philosopher, St Augustine of Hippo (354 -430 AD) had to give up upon this matter and quite plainly and bluntly concede out defeat upon this particular episode. The Christian church having based all the teaching over the element of truth had ended up preaching the biggest contradiction of all times. This church went even a step further as to categorically state that it had to be accepted and professed by every follower as a dogmatic sort of a truth, which must be rigorously upheld and be believed blindly in a most strict and diligent manner by all of its followers. No known society, or establishment could ever have survived after presenting such a bland and evident contradicting form of a fallacy by an establishment that had all along championed the 'Truth' as the emblem of its own foundation.

This church most bravely insisted that God is personalized in the image form of the Holy Trinity, but on the other hand had always been reluctant in order to accept the theory of evolution as had been presented out by Darwin.

The theory of evolution had been rejected because the Bible gives another version regarding our own kind of creation. The extract which deals over this subject is contained inside the episode of the Genesis, Chapter 2 vers 7, quote, 'And the Lord God found man of the dust of the GROUND and BREATHED into his nostril the BREADTH of life; and man became a living soul'.

Since all this information was being taken literally it must have given the impression that Adam our great, great g, g, „ father had been manufactured over a production line and his freckles should still be noticed whenever we take a bath. The Christian church must have concluded that Adam had been developed into a civilized, modern kind of a bloke in the stature of a 'Sir squire or a kind of a mister of a citizen of an Adam kind of a family'.

This church seemed to have overlooked the fact that

Adam is also an extended particle from our own Creator as had been proclaimed in various other parts of this holy book as well.

If this information has to be accepted thus it follows that we are all a trinity in the image of our Mentor who had created us in the first place.

Keeping all this information in mind we could now focus back over towards our organic structure once more.

The fact that we were transmitted over from a BREADTH gives us the impression that our gene must have been ignited out from a bacterial kind of a 'GERM'. This conclusion would eventually and effectively also alter the form of Darwin theory in order to regress such a claimed imaged forms of the apes into some form of a kind of a bacterial type of a 'GERM'. Breathing is a most effective way that germs and bacteria are spread around by us. Once that this process had been sparked out, than an evolutionary aspect was bound to ignite that must have spread out like wildfire.

It would have been most possible that 'hermaphrodites' would consequently evolve and be developed out by means of multiplying their quantities. These kinds of worms reproduce and multiply by a method of 'dissecting' from their own kind of a body. Even this process seemed to have taken place as well, when from the body of Adam had came around over here Eve.

How our other half came to be about is narrated in the Genesis Chapt 2 vers 21 - 22. 'And the Lord God caused a deep sleep to fall upon Adam and he slept; and he took one of his ribs and closed up the flesh instead thereof; 22

and the rib which the Lord had taken from man made him a woman and brought her unto the man'. Trailing further more along this line of thoughts should presents us with a vast amount of computations that could involve hybrids of tadpoles, frogs, snails and lizards out of which human kinds at some time or another had been 'vamped' out.

This DNA structure of our physical origin had been intersected with a pensive awareness that is also recorded inside the Holy Bible as well. Along the trail of human development our mind had embarked upon an unconventional path and due to this major kink that had deviated us away from these crawling models we had opened our eyes to accept that fruitful results are only made possible by means of sacrifices.

Out from a bipolar aspect our version had managed to obtain another leg and thus was 'deported' out from that singular stage that had no grades to assess our kinds.

The ideal example of a bipolar creature that graphically represent one single base over which it crawls and wriggle is best given out by an image of a serpent. The symbol of this creature had been chosen since it was deemed out to be the craftiest of these sorts of reptiles. Yet although this creature is known to be wise it is still attached towards the ground as in the ancient past.

These are some of the features that had been crucial towards the evolutionary aspects that had versed us towards this present sphere. A gate of existence was versed out when we had been able to grade the good and the bad.

It had been by the intuition of Eve that Adam was consequently involved with this experiment that is still an ongoing process since our physical impulses are currently being steered by our pensive means. This process that infused our nature kind had to start from a binary aspect of a simple device that had changed and altered in a decisive mode.

Out from a static and morbid state that had been rotating upon a calm and harmonious environment another sphere that was directed towards a serene and a relaxed habitat passed through a stage of a tempestuous and volatile form in a synchronized manner that is still evolving and revolving around this current type of a universe to these present days as well.

These had to be all the ingredients and qualities needed in order for this universe to be kept 'balanced, equated, matched and tuned' over the same habitat and environments of this current kind of an existing formation that we now have.

A state of enlightenment had been logged out from a dark stage.

Confirmation regarding all this computed details of positive and negative aspects could be noted out again from the Holy Bible just after Adam and Eve had sampled out the 'forbidden fruit'.

It was just after that stage that they had trespassed into this new domain and the characteristics of 'shame' had been impressed upon their heads which would have still had remained unknown if an opposite notion of 'pride' had not also been installed inside our 'lives' along as well. This elevated form of nature state had to be staged over a 'forked' phase that based intelligence over deleted bytes and invested wisdom out from previous forms of mistakes.

Pulses and impulses were invigorating nature forms to be managed by physical and pensive reflexes in order to steer and motivate us to enter into this current domain.

Prior to this stage existence was contained into a different sort of belt as far as our lives were concerned. After this episode they were aware of their 'entity' that had a 'personality' of a 'self' of a being and as such 'living' and 'existing' had 'modeled' out 'creation' to be completed out.

Body and mind were consequently managing 'cause and effect' directed out by concepts of our modes of perceptions and not vice versa. Their kind of nature forms had been upgraded by means of a process of demand and supply that were being rotating around them and thus encouraging and helping them to evolve all along by means of efforts and sacrifice and not drifting along existing forms.

Confirmation that these characters had managed to reach this stage could be noted when they went about to sew some clothing not because they were feeling cold but because they could conceive and perceive out their imaged formation since their eyes were opened up to face this current phase.

This information is presented out in the Holy Bible into the Gen 3 vers 7, along these lines, 'Then the eyes of both of them were opened and they realized that they were naked; so they sewed fig leaves together and made coverings for themselves'.

Polarity was the leading factor at this stage that was 'reflected' out by this current 'project' that had 'converted' out their manners by means of this new intentional 'mode of application' being installed in their nature frame.

It was during this current stage that thoughts of knowledge were composed over mistakes that were currently being made. It was also during this period that we had taken control of our 'nature forms' and steered these virtues and talents towards what we would want to perform.

Democracy was being fully exercised out since conceptions and perceptions were indiscriminately being used and utilized towards a finite aim of a 'pole' position performed out by the physical and the pensive sphere.

Perception and conception had been evolved and rotated over and around in a 'democratic' fashioned style being administered and governed out by us to 'gain knowledge and awareness'.

The physical and the pensive consciouses had evolved out of the swamps of the earth and thus volatile blood was in dire need to be covered or cleaned up from the mud out of which we had all came out from.

Hence this advanced level of both spiritual and organic state had to be redeemed and strained from both ends since our genes needed to exists and our lives longed and desired to enjoy what had been lost.

Having reached this present habitat that has positioned out our imaged form into this current stage we might try to confirm that we have not been stagnated out again into a circular kind of an existing sphere that has no finite aim. Once again our Mentor has furnished us with further signs that we are on the right track by:

(a) Establishing our image of a trinity just like Him by

inferring to Himself in the plural, and

(b) Presenting us with another version that is outside this existing living sphere.

These terms are lined up into these two sentences from the Holy Bible in Gen 3 vers 22, phrased thus, 'And the Lord God said 'The man has now become like one of Us, knowing good and evil. He must not be allowed to reach out his hand and take from the tree of life and eat, and live forever. '

The words good and evil confirms that the 'polarity' factor had been installed and so a terminal point had to catch up with our existing forms but our lives could never be harmed.

Even though we had been faced with extinction into our nature forms but our lives had been assured that they could survive for as long as we reach out for perfection through our existing phase.

Our ambitious nature had been given out a mission to accomplish, and our lives had been assured of eternal existence.

These objectives coupled by a finite aim could never be suggested out if our image had not been created in the likeness of an eternal being who had 'made' and 'created' us.

Various references could be given out to us to assure us that the Personality of God is imaged in the form of a Trinity.

A random spot check about when God had referred to Himself in the plural form is included down here although it might not be exhaustive:

1.   Gen 1. vers 26. Gen 3. vers 22. Gen 11 vers 8

2. The Transfiguration. Matthew 7. vers 1. -13.
3. The Baptism Luke 3. vers. 21. – 22.
4. The temptation. Luke 4. vers 1.- 13.

All of these quotes suggest that our existing kinds of nature forms are not to be considered out as being our lives, thus assuring us that another kingdom is in store waiting for us.

By means of those sorts of nature form that we all had inherited out from our own Creator we are presently able to hope that our end is not to be considered out as our terminal point.

Unfortunately there might be occasions when we would mistakenly regard out this 'existing' phase to be our 'lives' as well.

Whenever this attitude prevails we might again get immersed once more out from where we had originally came out before.

A clear description when we tend to be in danger of existing rather than living had been given out by Plato a Greek philosopher more than 2300 years ago.

He had managed to give a clear picture about our kind of 'nature forms' that we sometimes consider to be our lives when he narrated the episode of people scurrying around inside a subterranean cave chasing images and shadow forms.

These sorts of inclinations and orientations that could control our lives could blind us back again and retreat back from where we had came from.

This eternal struggle carried out in order to assures existence at the price of living is the first lesson given to us in the Genesis in chapter IV.

Along this episode is versed out an account when Cain had killed his brother Abel, because his offerings to God were not being welcomed just as much as those of his brother Abel were treated out.

This first murder recorded out into the Bible seems to have some connection with recent kind of archeological discoveries as well.

It is interesting to note that even a primitive line of creatures had been obliterated out as well for no apparent purpose or clear reason to be made. It has been found out that the primitive kinds of Neanderthals were wiped out some 40,000 years ago by their neighbors the Cro-Magnon in a similar manner as that of Abel. Even the ending of these two genocides seems to have the same pattern because Cain never admitted out any guilt and the archeologists have never been able to confirm that the Cro-Magnon had actually committed out this crime against the Neanderthals.

These two events had been brought forth in order to highlight out our nature forms that would confront each other to the point of extermination whenever care and affection are directed towards existence rather than living.

These existing nature forms that had enabled us to arrive here are also the beacons in order to transport us towards the next stage as these frames of syllogisms suggests here.

Wherever there is life there is hope.
Wherever there is hope there is a free will.
Wherever there is a will our reasoning are at the helm.
Wherever there is a target an aim can be made.

Wherever there is an aim an effort is at hand.
Wherever there is care then affection is also near.
Wherever there is affection along with care it gives us hope to return from where we came.

All these phrases would have no meaning if 'love' would be taken from their context.

Whilst some might agree with these suggestions there would be others who would rather look at the practical side of existence.

This is meant to happen every time we tackle 'love' since we either put it ahead of us or past our own sorts of lives.

This was the reason why the Christian church had got bogged into a literary trail, whilst the theory of evolution would keep presenting wider missing links to trace out our final genes.

The whole directorate of our existing catalogue tends to shield our roots and hides our 'nature forms' over images which alienates and deviate us from defining out exactly the origin that had initially sparked out our lives into existing.

This hide and seek process is clearly seen to take place whenever the origin of our kinds of 'nature forms' are being investigated out by us.

The same obstacles that impeded the Christian church and Darwin from coming to terms about defining out 'creation and origin' is still a major hurdle that is still kept under the carpet by society as well in present times.

A few experiences could be brought out to highlight the types of inclinations that bias our nature forms over either 'care' or 'affection' when a fruit of 'love' is born amongst us.

Most elderly people might recall how we were approached and treated when we got curious and inquired about from which state we had originally came to be around here. Although time have changed since those early days but the attitude that is presently being taken now is as strategically incorrect as had been some hundred years or so ago as well.

Parents in those days had always avoided from disclosing the carnal and sexual process that produce babies upon this earth. Whenever an explanation about our origin was given out it was normally based upon theological teaching rather than over an organic mode of a carnal aspect. Any kind of sex involvement was considered to be a taboo and was not to be mentioned let alone discussed around with children in those days. Some of us of a certain age may up to these very same day still recollect that we were told that 'Angels' from up yonder had brought us all down here, whilst other of a younger era might still remember how their parents used to tell them that a wonderful bird in the form of a stork had airlifted their kind of baby right inside the cozy comfortable cots which was always ready and handy in those bygone days. Later on when we where getting bigger and perhaps more brighter and therefore were becoming more inquisitive about these 'secrets' they had altered their version and made us believe that the particular midwife who had called around and had visited our home was the one responsible who had delivered over to us such a noisy bundle of joy inside her suitcase which she always used to carry around her.

Nowadays we do not need to do any further explanation any more because our children are being 'educating' in a formal manner about this subject in an institutional manner that is currently being based around the facts of life instead of fantasies.

Sex education is currently presenting our children with lots of information about the bare facts and figures that are involved and needed regarding the ingredients for us in order to make and fabricate out more 'babies' to exist. Only types of information and statistics are being presented to our children whilst an image form of 'affection versed over love' is nowhere to be found.

This attitude of getting swamped into 'facts and figures' was exactly what our elders along with Plato had dreaded since 'affection' tends to become a 'shadow'.

These kinds of flaws and mistakes would become more clear and obvious when they are being highlighted out towards case studies of extremes forms.

Thus we could clearly notice that children who had been deprived out from affection since they were young would concentrate their nature over logistics and statistics very 'carefully' in order to protect themselves from hazards. Their aptitude would take a cold streak whilst their affectionate character might hibernation. Their 'formation' would tend to be unreliable but their style would be very well developed to tackle 'existing' problems.

On the other hand those young children who had been spoiled with kindness might get the wrong impression about this existing phase and might expect living to be a garden full of roses. Their cultured live style would be well founded but if they should be faced with existing crisis they would be liable to break down easily.

In both these extreme cases the only medication that

could cure these ailment of heritage could only be found in 'love'.

This gift of 'love' had been the ingredient out from which we had all came out to exist over this current place here.

'Verbum Carum Factum Est'.

WHERE AM I?

The earliest attempt to audit out all the contents of this existing sphere were initially made at about 25000 years ago by Empedocles a philosopher living in Agrigento inside Sicily which in those days had formed part of the Greek colonies.

All the substances of this exiting sphere had been placed into just four items that were hailed out to be 'earth, fire, water and air' and unfortunately were understood to mean 'elements' and therefore were eventually discredited.

The contents of these four items holds the keys that are inscribed into their codes which could help us in order to 'define, state, dictate and explain' all the 'elements, forms, sorts and kinds' that are contained inside and around this existing frame of a universe.

Our own kinds of lives that are known to be an 'entity of a being that has a personality of a self ' have a residential place that is fashioned out to accommodate us exactly to suit the potentials that we have and possess.

Around these parameters has to be found our habitats and along this version we could be able to define our sorts of environments into which we are all contained.
Only upon this sort of a personal kind of a conduct could our versions be able to quantify and qualify anything that we could ever comprehend or understand over here.

Once again we have to resort towards our physical and

pensive frame in order to present and describe whatever these kinds could indicate out to us. This operation has to be managed by our pensive intentional modes of 'reflection, projection, application and inverting' over our sensual conducts of 'sight, digestion, feeling and auditing' that would present the bearings of the location of this current existing place over here.

This process that is meant to account for our own sorts of habitats has to be 'matched, balanced, equated and leveled' up with our current sorts of environments in order to be versed out over the appropriate belt of this existing kind of a universe.

Around these four digital spheres, states, stages and zones we could be able to locate the habitation that our kinds are presently living right now.

An overview of these aspects could only be made out whenever they could be screened from a conservatory that is detached and insulated out from these environments so that existence would not be considered out to be our kind of lives.

Along with this current version a hub has to rotate over an axle that has to be staged in the same manner as this universe revolves around us in order to note existing forms by means of the lives that we all have.

This aspect would prove to be the same as the potentials of our physical and pensive frame since they consternate and rotates just like this kind of a universe. Therefore if we should take everything into consideration it would result that our lives exists over features that are all synchronized just like the lives we have.

By means of this line of thinking we could be able to

define the habitat of our present kinds of environments into which we all live and exist.

Thus in order to take into account all the important information that had been given out so far, we could conclude that existing is composed into this quadrant version as indicated over here:

1. Entailed into a moments in time.
2. Are all related towards us.
3. Have a bearing upon us.
4. Are all composed of nature forms.

All these details could now be summed up into features that could be changed and altered into aspects that are crucial for existence to be complete. This quadrant frame that is contained into a synchronized version of four ranks could now be itemized out into these features here as well:

1. Time and space.
2. Relativity.
3. Polarity.
4. Matter.

This existing symphony could now be orchestrated over four platforms upon four different conduct of habitats that belts out our nature formations to correspond along with the varied types of environments that they regularly presents out to 'us'.

These four 'seasons' of different sorts of atmosphere rotates and changes in accordance to existing ambient that are all beyond our control.

Since we have to follow the conditions of these spheres thus we could never specify exactly the ambient that they currently hold.

Their overlapping nature forms makes it most difficult when a specific ambient finishes and another one start, but their resulting product gives out clear indications into which kind of habitat we are presently living now.

Hence these arbitrary states that contain overlapping stages between them could be organized out into these quadrant frames as explained over here;:

- A harmonious state would verse out a calm stage.
- A relaxed state would verse out a serene stage.
- A volatile state would verse out a tempestuous stage.
- A static state would verse out a morbid stage.

These environmental habitats all rotates and revolve around and over our lives and therefore their conditions could never be grasped by our potentials that have to rely and rest across their spheres.

On the other hand our potentials have to function upon them and so these features could be fractured out into existing 'elements' which we could describe since our lives are associated and linked to all of them.

A brief list that contains the profile of these existing factors could be made out in order give a short description of their conduct that they present out over to us.

- The factor of 'Matter' that had been imaged out as 'earth' has 'blue' pigments and is characterized out by a nature that cycles out forms.

- The factor of 'Relativity' that had been imaged out as 'air' has 'white' pigments and is characterized out by a nature of habitats that are located over here.
- The factor of 'Polarity' that had been imaged out as 'water' has 'green' pigments and is characterized out by a nature of production that generates this current sphere.
- The factor of 'Time and space' that had been imaged out as 'fire' has 'red' pigments and is characterized out by a twisting flame that we always try to avoid.

All of these aspects have qualities that are all similar to our physical and pensive potentials that controls out our existence but not the lives that we all have.

These four factors could very well be regarded out as the 'four corners of the world' that have been frequently mentioned in the Holy Scriptures as well.

These 'existing' forms could all be contrasted diagonally along with our kinds of 'lives' that should make it obvious that if a 'twist' is missing from one of them then our universe fall apart.

These 'crucial' factors of existence have these sorts of impact over our lives that sustain and support us by their current style, as explained over here:

1. We have a 'consuming' body that needs substances in the form of the element of 'matter'.
2. We have to 'relate' anything that we want to indicate out.
3. We have to push back in order to advance forward that makes the 'polarity' essential for all of us.
4. We record experience out of 'time and space' that

furnish us with a lease of grace in order to remember what had taken place.

These existing factors 'state, stage, pose and consternate' around us in the same manner as this whole kind of a universe that makes it obvious that our existence is related towards everything that happens over here.

The analogues of these sorts of similarities could enable us to locate exactly where our 'lives' are situated in this current form of an existing universe over here.

This existing place into which we are now lodged is opened wide to be investigated out by us since we had charted out the important features that could guide us to fathom out more this universe.

This exercise would be undertaken along the next four chapters that would treat out the 'factors of existence' individually, independently and exclusively by contrasting their potentials along with our own lives.

All of these factors are going to be analyzed so that their basic ingredients would come out forth as Empedocles had so wisely dictated so many years ago.

So after all these years 'earth, fire, water and air' are still as fresh to be examined again once more as when these 'elements' had been selected initially so many years ago.

MATTER

The rock, the wood, the glass, the stone
Are they the same as flesh and bone?
Is there some cycle that just goes round?
Returning oceans back into clouds!
Mother earth seems busy upon this quest
Calling back nature inside her own nest
All nature forms adopts this kind of sequence
That had been followed since the days of
      Mr. Homo sapience!

Matter is a virgin terrain that generates out everything over here.

The composition of this factor is imaged over a picture of this 'earth' out of which all sorts of tools and utilities are effectively being brought out forth.

All the substance and essence that could be described and defined out by our physical and pensive frame are contained and included inside the factor of 'matter' that is imaged out as the original ingredient of this current existing font out of which everything rotates. The roots of this factor would become evident to us whenever our methods of living initiate forward upon the image of this notch that upgrades our nature forms into a new sphere over the gradient of this current mode.

The personal aspects of the factor of matter are

contained into all sorts of ingredients that are over here that we all take for granted as a 'matter' of course.

The qualities of this factor are all the potentials that are gathered out into images that are regularly circulating around us.

This general overview about this nature form gives out the impression that this factor is the platform over which this kind of a universe is based upon. On the other hand since this version consists of just a frame, then the potentials and qualities that are contained inside it would all fade out if this textured form is isolated and left on its own.

Thus in order to explain out these kinds of factor a method of a synchronized fashion have to be adopted out in order to explain out properly these factors that eludes our grips but could be versed out from the shadow that they all leave behind them.

Therefore a pensive and a physical approach has to be made that would have to rotate over this form in order to present out a defined description over the conduct of this factor that is presently revolving around us all.

Anything that could be quantified and qualified over this kind of a version has to be gathered and contained into features of 'matter' and after that they could all be presented and explained upon this kind of a twisted trend.

Thus the imaged form of 'matter' kind has to supersede everything else in order to be versed out properly upon any form of a bench.

Therefore in order to go along with this line of thoughts the first kinds of details that are going to be given out have to be imaged out from the initial experiences that we had collected out as soon as we were all born over here.

This trail could commence from whence we had become aware of all the material aspect that we now have and posses.

Making acquaintances with our organs had been the first phase when we were confronted with 'matter' forms. Our initial lessons thought us to distinguish the difference between 'consumable' and 'tools' both of which are contained into the factor of 'matter' forms.

Normally it does not take very long for us in order to distinguish what is consumable, which are toys, who is me, and who are they over a rotary trend that has to be spun over the first impressions that we might have mistakenly made.

These sorts of primary lessons had upgraded us, since as soon as we tried to eat our tongue rather than to speak we must have grown to tell the difference there is between them, theirs and mine, as well as ours.

Along this trail of thoughts another bench had been reached which might have placed the factor of 'matter' form at the back since other 'features' would be highlighted out instead.

Our tongue might be used to sting someone else and our heart might also be given away to someone else whom we love as well. Even if we happen to graduate towards this elevated stage as soon as we tread over any new terrain 'matter' form has to lead our ways once more.

This sort of a graphic image of 'matter' forms explains how our mode of 'reflection' plays a major role that is constantly positioning this factor in front of everything else.

This current sequence is constant every time the frame of 'matter' is being tackled, since if other aspects block our sight then this ingredient would be cycled out and would be versed out into another format.

Therefore if 'matter' is to be highlighted out the platform of everything that supports what is to be explained cannot be altered or changed since the characteristics must always remain the same.

These are the current steps that have to be taken over which the factor of 'matter' should leave a mark for us to note the basic of ingredients contained inside this frame.

A. First all the details have to be gathered.
B. Secondly they have to be made useful to us.
C. Thirdly their aspect of utility would be described
D. Finally their represented version has to be changed and altered out into another stage of a different spectrum that would invert and convert them.

Over this type of a cyclic trend the factors of matter would become prominent and the other kinds of existing elements would all subscribe towards this mode to be highlighted by means of their kind of backings.

Along this chronological mode the factor of matter plays a major role since this style is synchronized and would present this particular format in the end.

This pattern cannot be flawed away from this fashioned style as otherwise the factor of matter would end up over at the back stage without giving it a chance to be highlighted in the end.

A spectrum of activities could be cited out upon this

factor that could highlight the importance of matter forms that always sustain and supports out our lives.

We could all log these kinds of details that should always initiate over a new page in our style of current live we all lead in order to be focused over this mode. Some examples that we might cite for these impressions to be imaged out by us could be made whenever we embark to make a speech, planting out seeds into a pot or perhaps inviting out guests for a party and even meeting new members, as well as noticing the morning mist as we get up regularly from out of our beds.

These imaged forms of 'matter' are regularly changing round but the qualities are always being contained along the trend of substance and essence that would always leave a shadowed image of a formation that would always be left out behind.

Matter forms are managed and directed over this synchronized mode that has to go astride with our kinds of lives upon a current bench in order to avoid discrepancies to happen or occur that would unbalance out this existing sphere. Once our sphere is organized over a regulated frame then creation could exist over a harmonious stage over here.

Whenever the pattern designed for 'matter' forms is hurried or rushed faster than our lives could keep pace with them than catastrophic abnormalities are bound to occur that would always disorientate our lives away.

Some examples could be described that are not being aligned with our current lives that we normally lead now. One case in point is those new products that are now being produced out in a rush and are not following a natural trend along our organic living fashioned style.

These forms might take the images of food, cash, marriages, politics or anything else that are scurrying away differently than us and so anomalies could be noted out from the results that these versions would always leave behind.

All these 'material' forms that are not astride with our lives tends to change our nature forms in a drastic modes because their 'organized' style is different than our.

The general image of the version of matter form is normally represented out by the status of mother kind symbol. The reason for this conception could be that our pensive and physical means were given out from our own kinds of mothers and thus we tend to look upon her as the storekeeper of this kind of a universe who supplies the initial ingredients imaged out as 'matter' forms. Hence the characteristics of this factor are presently focused upon a mother image that might change if our personalities would be altered out from the way babies are being born now.

Apart from our own personal forms of organs even data and information could be contained into an image form of 'matter' for as long as they are being considered out as useful details and not just as forms of bytes whenever 'information' is the topic on the agenda being treated out by us.

Whenever this conception is being staged first, then forms of details might be brought to occupy the center stage and the subject of 'use and utilities' would take their place and this point would be placed somewhere else. Even if our own personal sorts of programming in life, is to concentrate over the factor of 'matter' then we have to focus upon this mode and ignore the features of cause that are regularly being reflected out from the content of this frame.

The images of matter could also be cited out in forms of cash whenever these are considered to be tokens over which we have to survive. These kinds of talents that had graduated along with prostitution have transformed their status and have a long history attached against their name.

The form of money that must have been imaged out by the utilities of the wooden stick have by now been changed into plastic cards and might even end up into just prints out from our own kinds of hands as well. Over every sphere whenever money is being regarded and treated out as something new to us then these kinds of tokens would be leading us over another bench to asses out a better meaning of these sorts of talent kinds.

Matter in a tangible state is imaged out as those kinds of tokens that establish out our current stature. They sustain, help, assist and support our make in order to do, act, perform or compose everything upon which we have to live and exist. Matter could take the image of food, a car, people or even a hand that would encourage us to scout new grounds that were unknown before to us. All these sorts of examples have to be set over virgin terrain in order for 'matter' to come out in front of the other kinds of 'elements'.

The ancient imaged version of the cart and donkey have by now been transformed into a car and the crop of our harvest are by now contained into the weekly pay packet that we might expect regularly to be cashed into our pocket by most of us. All these sorts of rituals are liable to transport us over another plan whenever we get bored and change them over some new terrain that would eventually be used to explore new grounds again.

Even the old style of bartering that is now being represented out by business deal has now been changed from its original image since the factor of money had also altered its form as well. The image form of money that is based over coin token models has carried these same kinds of ingredients for a very long period over here. It is interesting to note that gold, silver, gems and emeralds are still in demand because their forms takes a longer time to change and alter and therefore they retain their initial status more than other kinds of elements since they do not corrode so easily and so their images are still in the limelight. These forms of talents kinds that might have emerged out from the form of a pebble or a wooded club have changed their image forms into money types that are vital and crucial for us to be sustained and also in order to survive.

Nature has provided us all with ample amount of substance and products so as to practice and train upon these kinds of matter format in order to maintain and retain our kind of formations over which we revolve into various other spheres by using and utilizing them all over here.

After we 'log' over matter form this factor would dissolve into an existing particle and would be contained into a 'capsule' that might be 'used and utilized' over this 'page'.

Matter is as prominent in the pensive field just as much as the physical sphere.

Mental stress and pressures that we might have to endure could all be the results of disappointments and expectations that we all have composed beforehand. These mental aspects are all matter form that have all changed and altered along our current lives but their imaged shadows could be seen being reflected out over us since our version is finding it difficult to adapt to another new material mode.

Various sorts of rules and regulation upon which our lives are being led could all be traced backwards towards a stage in which they all had 'mattered' out more to us than they might all presently be right now.

Some forms of rules and legislations have grown so old as to have by now done their full cycle and needs new 'material' to be organized into them once more. Different examples could be cited out ranging out from those kinds of 'health and safety' regulations that some of them might have elapsed, along with some crazy notices that are prohibiting us from feeding pigeons that are starving in urban towns. At various times our human version seems to go down a 'peg' or two from this stage that should always commence out from everything that really and actually 'matters' out to all of us.

The most recent problem regarding our lives at present times is an environmental issue about the ozone layer.

It is very strange that some nations are not doing their best to solve this vital problem.

These papers have already pointed out the sorts of abnormalities that would result when existing forms are not organized in line with our current lives that we presently have and possess.

Whenever this alignment is lost catastrophic events are bound to occur since 'matter' forms could not support and sustain the current lives we have.

Future kinds of more evolved generation than us might look upon this sort of a mistake in the manner as if someone is burning a wooden shed in order to warm the feet and has forgotten to cover up the head!

The factor of matter that regularly presents us with newer version to generate our selves gives us an opportunity in order to reflect, monitor and screen whatever is to occur next.

In the same manner as when the high priest shred up his clothes in order to shed the garments of a novice our 'high' society would do likewise if the features of 'matter' forms are not handled with due care for all of us to enjoy. The kind of kicks and twists that we all get out of this imaged form, is that it revolves and recycles all of us, which unequivocally confirms exactly what Empedocles of Sicily had once said, that 'earth' is an 'element' over which existence is based.

'Matter' - initiate out nature forms.

TIME AND SPACE

How long has it been since we came here!
A whole life time, or somewhere near!
We're made a unit, a shape a mould
That ages by time, and so gets old!

We'll stop this ticking and jam that hand
just put a light bulb where the sun hangs
All past and future needs not apply
And if someone asks we'd all reply

'Must have been there since don't know when,
you had better ask,
                    Homo Sapiens'

The fashion of time and space could only be attributed to 'here and now', after this version had been altered and changed to become in line with our living phase so as to indicate out exactly and precisely what had been meant whenever it is being expressed.

'Here and now' are always being described out from 'there and then' since by the time it takes to explain them, they would always drift and be displaced and misplaced somewhere else. This is what always happen and occur whenever we log into these nature forms that cannot be restrained and kept into logical terms by means of our current kind of an organic frame that alters and change.

This eloping image is consequently being distorted out by means of the past tense along with the future sphere that makes us all believe that 'here and now' is in fact what had been phased out a moment ago over 'there and then' across a lateral sphere.

Therefore since any direct approach cannot be made to explain this current phase, a different strategy has to be adopted so as to tackle this current version that is presently going to be handled now.

The same pattern that had been used for the factor of 'matter' is going to again going to be used again but the chronological order is going to be changed out this time. Hence the same sentences are going to be used once more but the sequence has got to go along this frame instead;-

A. First their represented version has to be changed and altered out into another stage of a different spectrum that would invert and convert them.
B. Secondly their aspect of utility would be described.
C. Then they have to be made useful to us.
D. Finally all the details have to be gathered.

In order to locate this island out from this flowing stream, we have to begin out from 'there' in order to get over 'here'. Over this same bench whatever we might be considering as being 'now ' has got to be situated away from what had been elapsed and be reversed upon what is in actual fact presently 'staged'.

After we locate the exact habitat into which we presently are, then we could synchronize the actual timing of 'now' as well.

Thus in order to zero upon this current place over 'here' first, we have to 'equate, balance, match and twin' up this atmosphere that would change and alter this present kind of environment into cold statistics instead of events.

Hence all these forms of statistics of just types of utilities have got to be transformed into useful means in order to comply with the next line of the sentences that contains instructions in order to locate exactly where is 'here'.

Effectively these kinds of statistics would have to be changed and altered into various kinds of situations so as to indicate the position into which we all are now 'staged'.

Thus all the varieties of situations that we might have experience inside this world could all be recalled out as forms of 'expectations, anticipation, disappointments as well as celebrations' that we must have experienced over here.

So now if all these images could be calculated out and measured how far away they are from the 'ideal' state that we all wish and desire to be now we could be able to locate our position in relation to this optimum stage that we know exactly what it contains.

Therefore if a harmonious situation has to be selected out as a strategic aspect over which we could stage whatever we had expressed, then we could all calculate how far away we are distanced away from this static position of an ideal sphere that should indicate out exactly where we are presently 'staged' now.

After having used this 'flame' as a refrigerant, now we could have a look at the hot soot that are always left behind whenever any kinds of fire dies out.

By means of using the same facilities that had been crucial for us to locate out our actual position over here, these same potentials could now be switched over into various kinds of ambient and spheres over which we could zoom and adjust out our clock as well.

The various kinds of situations of 'expectations, anticipations, disappointments and celebrations' that were all used to find out our present place by noting how far away we are from it, have now got to be transformed out into seasons instead of events in this case now.

So different types of different seasons have got to take the places of events and therefore these have got to be transformed into versions of habitats now instead. So these metered formations would contain different sorts of ambient instead of events.

Hence these rotating kinds of four seasons could start from a calm stage of a tranquil mode that might alter into a relaxed sphere being staged into a serene type that might turn into a morbid state of a static formation which might again surf up into a violent state over a tempestuous ambient that would switch over another kind of a foreign plane as well.

These circular patterns are endured by all of us over a style that rhymes with the fashion of our personal lives that matures and transforms all of us over different 'vibes' that have to 'pulsate' along with our lives that consequently change and alter us.

Thus by means of noting the pulsation of our nature forms we could note whether our existing forms are astride and synchronized with our current lives or not. By means of regulating our pulses along a perfect atmosphere over a perfect state, then our kind of timings would have to be considered out to be precise and exact for us right 'now'. Any perfect ambient that we had missed or we intend to reach is an exact time that suits us so the time right now must relate towards that focal spot that is regulating our watch.

All these points have been presented out by means of anomalies or discrepancies matched along our current sorts of lives that we have.

A synchronized state of 'here and now' could only be graded and assessed precisely by us, for as long as we could note out exactly what is happening over 'there' and 'then'.

Once again our own kinds of personal nature forms are being held responsible for informing us by means of wisdom and intelligence that have proven to be crucial ingredients to recognize the flame of 'time and space' as well.

The recording instruments that had been utilized in order to describe out the factor of 'time and space' had been the pensive and physical potentials that we all have. Both of these kinds of utilities have developed and advanced us all considerable well and subsequently we have managed to fathom out towards perfection that is always a challenge for all those who wants to be more precise and exact.

These modes of perceptions and conceptions had consequently evolved and developed because we had shown affection, care and respect towards everything that is currently over here.

Thus a mode of conceptions over perceptions could be used to indicate out our present timing that could be synchronized over the pulses of others by which we could regulate out our own personal clock towards a model of perfection so long as we care to adjust whatever we could note to be at fault.

A form of timing could always be adjusted out better still whenever we strive for higher virtues that could transport us from across this barring fence and position us over 'here and now' that could only be made possible if we accept that we are always being 'there and then'.

'Here and now' could be distorted and changed over any sort of a rotary frame that we might like to select for our lives to follow and as such we might end up into different grounds over various times as well.

These distorted line of thinking could be based upon imaginary spheres that would conduct anachronisms being brought forward into different kinds of ambient that are unknown by us. This is the reason why imagination has no boundaries since the components that are involved are elastic kinds of 'mortals' that are fashioned and styled out from flexible kinds of clay that have no specific form.

Programming, planning, expectations and anticipations are never precise and therefore an exact time could not be versed over anything that keeps changing and alternating upon this kind of an atmosphere. Only a morbid frame composed over rigid statistics that are impeded from evolving out any more could locate a stationary place staged over here.

All these detailed information have surfed since the instructions of the prescribed pattern had been followed out correctly, as otherwise the objective would been changed into studying the ingredients of a clock or on the other hand looking at the stars out from a holed spot relating out whatever had been staged out before.

These sorts of mistakes could be amplified if the 'pattern' was not followed out correctly.

In order to prove this point two examples could be cited out when the instructions of the patter had been misplaced and displaced out from their chronological set order.

An old example had been made in the form of a story that has remained as a memorable kind of paradox regarding spaced timings is attributed to Zeno of Elea 450 BC, who had composed that famous tale about a race between Achilles and the Tortoise.

This fable is about a race between a fleeting Achilles and a slow moving Tortoise that could never be won by Achilles since the little advantage that was initially given out towards the Tortoise could never be written off.

This situation was kept unchanged because their 'metered' utilities were never made out useful to 'contrast' over a common bench and so their individual 'details were not gathered' but were kept 'to represent out them'.

They were never given out a chance to change the initial ambient upon which they had begun and started the race so their own 'seasons' never integrated since their potentials were kept at bay by being halved without giving them a chance to overlap.

Should this story had been followed along the guidelines given out by the suggested pattern in these papers, than the results could have been versed out differently if their utilities had been given out a chance to alternate at a finite stage when the ingredients had been 'gathered' after they were 'converted' out.

On the other side of the coin our position that relates towards the ingredients of time and space had been treated out by the theory of relativity that was defined out into statistics of, $E = mc2$ recently by Einstein during the last century.

This theory has been computed out to suggest that 'time and space' could flow ahead or backward once again.

A lot of controversy has came out from this theory that gives out the impression that forms of explosive stars are ahead of our time whilst spectrum of black holes holds a secluded past inside all of them.

These 'aspects' are true within the 'three dimensional' of relativity but their 'utilities' could never overlap the 'season' into which there are held and so their quadrant features would always be kept 'framed' away from us.

Although the present perfect state is a 'quadrant' frame directing and managing this 'case' could only be made upon a triangular 'point' or over a 'hexagon' in order to prove that this 'matter' of 'time and space' 'relates' back to us whatever had been said by us in a 'pole' position in the first place.

Perceptions and conceptions could be equated out into this 'frame', but we could never be left out.

This illusive flame could only give up an amount of 'heat' for us long as our temperature is colder than the temperature that is currently being given out by this burning tongue.

Once again Empedocles had managed to discover the emblem of 'time and space' before us when he had suggested out that 'fire' is a finite kind of an 'element'. 'Time and space' - infuse out a current system.

RELATIVITY

The length and breadth the width and weight
What have they in common with small or great?
Large is bigger than you have thought!
Whilst small is always tiny, next to naught.
So! Are we the middle of 'an in between'?
Of this great cosmos, that's what it seems!
For if a whole is equal to just one 'man'
then everything else, is in relation to
                        Homo Sapience!

A 'mean' gradient upon which 'relativity' had been applied universally had originated from the personal 'organs' that we all have and possess whenever we try to describe out anything between 'us'.

It was Protagoras of Abdera a Greek philosopher who had lived between 489 and 411 BC, who had noted out this trend amongst us, and made that memorable statement that 'Man is the measure of all things'.

On the other hand the nature form of 'relativity' when detached away from 'us' could only be imaged out into the symbolic form of 'air', which once more proves Empedocles was right again.

Thus stating out this 'environmental ambient' has to be 'graded, quantified, qualified and assessed' out by us and versed out again within this existing sphere as well.

Therefore the same form of a tabled pattern that had

been drafted out before is going to be used here once more, but the chronological order is going to be changed in order to give prominence towards this factor that is presently being treated out now.

Hence the same sentences are going to be used once again but the sequence is now changed along this frame instead;-

A. Everything around us has to be made useful to us.
B. Then all the details have to be gathered.
C. Their represented versions have to be changed and altered out into another stage of a different spectrum that would invert and convert them.
D. Finally their aspects of utilities have got to be described.

Everything that is around us consists of 'sorts, types, kinds and forms' that supports and sustains us all to perform, conduct, direct and evolve over this sphere.

So if all these sorts of utilities have got to be described out from us, we all have to act out as agents as well as the types of ingredients over which we would have to invoice out whatever might represents out 'us' in order to be composed in the end.

Therefore all of these details would be transferred over latent 'grades, qualities, means, and tokens' that in the end would all be transferred back into various modes to be exchanged and organized by us upon a common benchmark hof our lives.

Accordingly tangible example has to be made out now in order to lace up this stated pattern so as to give a current picture of its form.

Examples that could be presented out in order to view out this 'factor' in a very prominent way are the current sorts of business deals and transaction that we do regularly in a methodical way between all of us.

On every occasion whether we buy or sell various kinds of goods a dimension of 'weights, measures, qualities and quantities' have to relate a stable mode in order to represent out a spectrum of cash that would eventually change hands over a benchmark that has to be accepted from both ends.

This accepted benchmark of a prescribed dimension must always be 'equated, matched, leveled and twinned' up over tokens of efforts and sacrifices when they exchange hands between us.

Thus over one side of the scale cash money had been equated out over means of sacrifice whilst at the other end various wares were graded, calculated and assessed over different dimensions that had to relate with our organs in the first place.

We might still trace out some of these original dimensions that had been extracted out from 'us' and had been used out as 'agents' over which business transaction could never have ever been made in the first place.

So if for an example in the past we had required any length of an 8 inches long we had to ask for a 'span' to be ordered over that current bench in those bygone days, and if that was not enough then a 'foot' which we are still considering to measure out '12 inches' might have been enough.

All of these kinds of 'agents' that had been useful yesterday would eventually be extinct since precision would be more crucial for transactions to be made,

Few might remember that in the olden days when someone used to order out an amount of a 'bath' of fluid it used to be assumed to contain about 5 gallons liquid which must have been considered to be the enough for a person to get a proper wash.

Without these sorts of 'agents' no business transaction could ever have been aired out, since no form of invoicing could have been possible to be framed out. By means of these current forms of commissioned 'agents' invoices could be presented out in order to finalize out any sort of transaction to be contracted out over a chart that relates what had been agreed beforehand.

Every sort of a business deal has to be 'aired' out first in order take place.

These 'agents' that relates a 'perceived concept' between us is vital for our own existence to evolve.

The importance of these current 'agents' that we regularly us is commonly noted out every time a traffic incident is contested out.

Only a stable image could ever vouch who had eventually moved towards the other item involved and so in this case the shadow of a 'witness' is once again an important agent that could be used to establish out who had caused that crash to happen.

If relativity could not be handled and controlled out by us, we could either never stop eating or else would not be able to relate whenever we get hungry and so would starve to death.

There was also a phase when humanity was insensitive towards the symptoms of this current factor and consequently our knowledge and awareness were in danger to be suffocated since they were kept suppressed and never given out fresh 'air' to develop out more.

A clear example when these events were occurring over here was when Nicolas Copernicus the Prussian astronomer (1473 – 1543) as well as Galileo Galilei (1564 – 1642) could not be able to express their views to describe out better our kind of a universe.

Humanity was compelled to change the current views that the earth was not the center of this whole universe because 'most useful' items in those days were being related over towards the 'sun' that was a vital spectrum upon which everything could be related out from the image that it conveyed upon us in those days.

The imaged formation of the sun during those days was a stable factor in order to gauge time, harvest crop and locate positions over and upon the bearings taken as a mean to measure out 'everything' that was considered to be useful in those bygone days. So it should come as no big surprise that some civilizations had also considered the image of the 'sun' as to be their 'god', since all their useful issues all related towards this symbol that was so crucial to them.

These types of shadow could be noticed switching and changing around us as well whenever codes of ethics replaces moral values and religious teachings are transferred into codes of ethics.

Since the factor of relativity is the 'rock' over which our bearings could be noted out then if our orientations and inclinations would loose the meaning of 'love' we tend to get lost for directions of what is right or wrong.

Certain values that might have meant a lot for our ancestors in bygone days might be regarded out now as being silly or useless for us presently, whilst whatever we might consider now as being serious or vulnerable could have been seen as vulgar or even insulting many a moons ago.

The importance for our means of existence is always being gauged upon the ratio over which our reasons values the substances that are essentials for us to live in the long term.

Family relationship is the greatest challenge every time this factor is being contested during breakdown of marriages.

Since the fulcrum of this factor always pivots upon the ingredients of the nature of 'love' then the culprit for this impact could only have been responsible by the party that showed less 'care' into this bondage.

The terms 'for better or for worse' should never ever contain small prints since eventually they would have to be described and explained out every time a marriage breaks up.

The nature of communication in every field validates the ingredients of relativity upon a spectrum that inverts whatever had been expressed upon 'features' that are common to both ends, after they had been converted out from a 'station' that had transmitted them out in the first place. On the other hand all types of dialects develop out from a language that had been deflected because essential terms were needed to express out new information being important to be described out more precise.

All of these types of synchronized aspects relates out an essential bearings over which we all have to regulate our lives in order to exist upon this current bench here.

Whenever we are tempted to relate out different kinds of weights and measures in order to take existing advantage out of this factor through means of cheating than our own kinds of lives are the ones that would end up being deprived in the end.

Lack of honesty would eventually make us change our own personal concepts and would effectively make us loose direction of what is best even for ourselves.

Should these warning signs be ignored then we tend to become self centered and treat our 'ego' as our own type of God.

We are all free to relate upon a stable 'rock' that could be 'measured and assessed' by our means and 'aired' out in order to be defined and described.

'Relativity' - organize out an ambient.

POLARITY

The north has south
The east has west
The top has bottom
What about the rest.
The good has bad
We all know that.
But what's wrong with a heaven
Without, that damned hell?
Can't we just have gain
Without any sort of pain?
Bet this been tried over and over again,
Must surely have tired out,
That poor old creature of a,
Homo Sapience

The features of the polarity factors are lined without any sort of an understatement being endorsed into or along this mode.

This diagonal aspect has a latent form that streak past our mortal kinds since we could never grasp any term that is singular positive or just negative for as long as we are grounded inside this universe.

Subsequently perfection would remain foreign to us, and 'good or bad' cannot ever be expressed if not 'termed' with an opposing element to support whatever has to be claimed.

Any concept of a perfect content that is believed out to be exact and precise would always fade and be blanketed away just as soon as we gauge and meter it out into any finite test.

Even items that we deem out to be as 'diligent, decent, straight and honest' had to rest over and upon 'kinked, strange, weird, or grotesque ' formation before they could ever be graded out as such by 'us'.

Along these parallel aspects of lateral forms could be imaged a 'pole' position that has a target without an aim and tends to race upon a single leg in order to image this factor inside its virgin state.

The profile of this factor cannot be contained since a shadow of this aspect would change the form of this element into a 'term'.

Only upon these guidelines and directions could we be able to assess and grade those elusive elements of positive and negative trends that are 'known' by all of us but could never be extracted out into a finite mode.

Hence in order to view out this transparent factor of a translucent formation these elements have to become 'opaque, cracked, mistaken or smudged' inside their nature so that a shadow of their image would surf up.

Subsequently over this cloudy spectrum we have to embark in order to define out what cannot ever be found over here, and upon these shadowed images we have to define and phrase out a 'dead' end.

This impossible mission is meant to define out positive element into a finite term and has to phrase out an extinct negative formation inside an existing mode.

This task is now made easier since the model for the 'pattern' that had been used to extract the former factors could now be used and utilized by its last form of a computed version now.

Hence these elements that are beyond and above our means should all be presented out forth if the instructions of the pattern would direct this process to be effectively performed.

Along this trail of deduction we can now proceed to compose the chronological order of the next pattern that could only be staged over its final computed style now. So the same sentences are going to be phrased out but they are now positioned differently along this manner and so these elusive elements should now end up being 'made useful to us'.

A. All aspects of utilities have to be described out.
B. Their represented out versions have to be changed and altered out into another stage of a different spectrum that would invert and convert them.
C. Then all the details have to be gathered.
D. Finally everything around us has to be made useful to us.

Consequently then if every sort of utility has to be inspected out by us they have to be classified out into 'energy, force, discourse, and resource'.

Conversely if we have to treat out all these useful amenities respectively they have to be tackled out by our 'self, entity, person and being' in order to be 'justified, quantified, qualified and be defined' out by 'us'.

In order to voice out any amount of debacles out of these sorts of ingredients a form of resistance has to be made out so as to emulate out any type of response being tuned out whenever these items are contrasted or confronted along with our sorts of lives we have.

Now that a graphic image of this spectrum of utilities had been penciled and bundled up into a uniform code we could be able to study these shadowed images over their 'pole' position whenever they are back or in front of our kinds of lives that we currently have and possess over here.

Thus in order to explain a comprehensive meaning out from the features of this factor all the essentials kinds of utilities have to be contrasted out along with a spectrum of our own lives in order to find out the meanings of those unqualified phrases that we all dish out whenever we tend to define these unknown 'elements'.

Subsequently another tabled form has to be laid out in order to emulate out different terms of positive kinds of elements to be unequivocally phrased out from the compendium of our own sorts of personal lives that we have along these lines:

- Anything that has to feature out as 'just and right' for us could only be defined out exactly by our own kind of 'entity' that is qualified to term this phrase upon a rhetoric form of a logical mode.
- Anything that has to feature out as 'correct and perfect' for us could only be defined out exactly by our own kind of 'being' that is qualified to term this phrase upon what is staged over here.
- Anything that has to feature out as 'organized and precise' for us could only be defined out exactly by our own kind of 'self' that is qualified to term this phrase upon a synchronized aspect that is finite.

- Anything that has to feature out as 'best and vital' for us could only be defined out by our kinds of 'personalities' that owns the necessary potentials to gauge and asses these nature forms.

All of these capsules of positive elements had been defined over statistics that were all 'equated, balanced, twinned and leveled' up with our own sorts of lives and therefore cannot be challenged or contested out in any existing mode since 'we' had announced their 'finite' lines.

All of these shadowed images of a positive term could now be positioned out into an inverted spectrum of an 'opaque, cracked, stained or crashed' formation that should present out a negative image over their kinds instead.

Consequently these obscure profiles have to be brought forth in order to account for their respective elements of a negative aspect now instead.

Hence these images have to be presented out over a common bench but must be tainted instead.

A negative aspect has been highlighted out by these four sentences along these inscribed lines over here:

- Any image of an opaque kind of nature in our lives is modeled out whenever we are branded or discriminated in any way.
- Any image of a cracked kind of nature in our lives is modeled out whenever we endure any mistakes upon us.
- Any image of a stained kind of nature in our lives is modeled out whenever we are being exploited out in any form.

- Any image of a crashed kind of nature in our lives is modeled out whenever we are used and abused by means of other kinds like us.

All these versions could now be forwarded out as contents of liabilities upon which could be assessed the properties of a negative element to be presented out as a defined mode.

These models could now be fashioned out along a designed role to be itemized out accordingly this way;-
Items that are opaque are always viewed with suspicious just because their intentions, motifs, objectives or targets are forms of elements that are obscure to us.

Items that are cracked could in most elementary cases be mended or repaired, scraped or altered as in every mistake incurred by anyone of us.

Items that are stained have their elements smudged because other kinds are more competitive, better, superior or greater than the one who is always left behind.

Items that are crashed into gravels or crystal, bits or bytes are all elements that are used to construct, build, plan or program another page into the chapter of our current lives we have.

All of these terminal phrases had been greeted with a superior amount of resistance that had burnt up all the contents of any positive particle to be found and as such we have to conclude that this kind of a fuselage is a definite element of a negative format.

These same pensive elements had been aptly proclaimed out by professor Edward de Bono (lateral thinking 1969) as 'what is left when something happens and does not completely unhappen'. On the other hand the potentials of this factor could be noticed inside an electric singular pole conduct on its own form.

Although modern technology had managed to amplify the polarity factor into amounts of 'volts, watts, amps and current' that flow unnoticed around our homes, yet the actual light of this factor had been given out to us by Empedocles of Sicily when he had selected out 'water' as a basic element.

He had successfully managed to synchronize this universe by baptizing this existing sphere with 'water'.

'Polarity' - stage out a new position.

WHO AM I?

In order to define out exactly my kind of 'being' the 'personality of the entity of my self' have to be brought around to vouch for 'me'.

My own profile would be complete for as long as all my characteristics are presented out in order to describe correctly 'who am I'.

We might be satisfied with various kinds of 'labels, tags, brands or titles' that we all carry about in the manner of effigies that are indexed in order to be classified to be prepared for the next roll call to be made.

All of these nomenclatures or adjectives might represent our imaged shadows but these sorts of nom de plumes cannot ever be regarded out to be the kinds of lives that we all have.

These imaged features are most important in order to index and classify out our nature forms but unfortunately these sorts of credentials could never be assumed to have any kind of a relationship with the lives that we have and possess.

The qualities of our lives could be totally different from whatever our name might dictate, and when our kind could not keep up with the gauged standard of our name then we might end 'living' up for our featured name and our own lives would end up being screened in the past.

An ailment of an identity crisis would always trouble

our lives whenever a form of a mask would take over our personal image instead.

Whenever we tend to reject out our own personal means, than we might adopt another existing 'form' but would always be let down every time we ask 'who am I'.

Aesthetic images of attractive forms are most desired by all of us but discarding the fibers that had wound up our initial frame render us a spectrum void of any type of heritage.

Whenever existing is being considered out to be more important than living than our form tends to loose contact with the genes of heritage out of which we had all originally came.

Different sorts of examples could be cited out when these kinds of strings of heritage had been broken and the cords that were linked to our ancestors had left no mark for future generations to trace out their genes, due to this synthetic line that had sterilized their image inside a dream.

Some characters might try to do their utmost to keep their lives attached to an effigy that had long been burnt out from them, whilst other would never accept the fact that their fiery pep had long departed their nature forms although they keep on scratching wax to kindle what had long run dry. Botox cream might do the job in order to hide the wrinkles whilst 'toys of guys and dolls' could keep some characters dreaming on a little more until they look into the mirror and find out that a stranger has lodged amongst them.

All these sorts of apprehensions might not be aligned or synchronized upon the current abilities that our lives have or possess and therefore an identity crisis of some form would have to be covered or masked up away from them.

Some might do their best to be turned into a rainbow, whilst other would make sure that their shadowed spectrum would stay locked and hidden inside a closet away from all of them.

These kinds of human mistakes are regularly being adjusted out by us every time we tend to chew up more than we could munch and therefore we are constantly discovering out our existing forms of abilities and capacities that are regularly positioning out our lives upon a chart of an organic font.

Over and upon this current benchmark we could gather out all the necessary 'oats' to bale out a proper name that has to be respected out by everyone since the godfathers are going to be chosen and selected out from 'us'.

Thus in order to select, grade, assess and define out an identity that would prove to be beyond reproach it has to be 'announced, hailed, expressed and composed' out from our lives in order to suit 'us'.

Our personal abilities over which we could diagnose out any existing form could only be carried out by means of our senses of 'tasting, feeling, hearing or seeing' which have to be sorted out upon the modes of 'reflecting, projecting, application or converting' in order to be zoomed and presented out as a conduct of our lives. These are the chromosomes of our own lives being equivalent towards the DNA structure of our blood cells and should they be altered and changed out then our kinds would become foreign and alien to what we are now.

Across this panel of a quadrant mode we could be able to construct a proper identity that would suit us whenever it is being hailed out.

This inscribed term of our sorts of personalities has to be laced over what we currently own and posses.

Hence our own formation has to be stripped out bare in order to grade out the details of our own sorts of finite elements that we all have.

This process could be conducted out along these lines here:

- Any person is complete if it consists of a 'being, entity and a self'.
- Any being is complete if it consists of a 'self, person and an entity'.
- Any self is complete if it consists of an, 'entity, being and a person'.
- Any entity is complete if it consists of a 'person, self and a being'.

Consequently an existing 'cube' had been inverted and converted out into a 'tripod' that in each and every case it had been portrayed, projected and framed out from us.

Thus an existing aspect had consequently been transformed out into a variety of chromosomes upon which we could now be able to construct out a version that is certified to be true and correct since it is going be composed out of those personal loops that all had initially been extracted out from us.

This kind of a birth certificate has all the necessary ingredients upon which we could now phrase out the qualities that we all possess but an appropriate modem upon which this cleavage has to rest has still got to be tracked and traced out as well by 'us'.

This 'peerage' upon which we could anchor all our existing credentials have got to be extracted out from nature forms that are all around us over here.

So if our own 'lives' have got to be graded out through the pulses of existing features then these 'concepts' have to be perceived out by us as well.

These pensive modems could all be described out by us through these methods here:

- Our kind of a 'being' is currently modeled out from the contents of 'space and time' to be reflected over her.
- Our kind of an 'entity' is currently modeled out from the contents of 'relativity' to be applied over.
- Our kind of a 'self' is currently modeled out from the contents of 'polarity' to be projected over here.
- Our kind of a 'person' is currently modeled out from the contents of 'matter' to be versed out inversely over here.

Now upon this bench we could categorically suggest that this professed standard is the basic grade that would exactly identify out a version of the present kind 'Homo Sapience'.

Should we be satisfied over this primary stage then 'existing' forms would have to be considered and treated out to be as our type of 'gods'.

When this attitude prevails 'mother nature' is the mentor of primitive culture whilst modern personalities chase an elixir of illusions.

In extreme cases that we change our present 'image' then our form could also become foreign to us as well.

This is when 'living' and 'existing' presents us with a crisis that could not loop up over our personal type of an 'identity' that we have and posses.

Our present personal bench mark has currently evolved to a standard that could tell the difference between a living phase to exist and an existing image.

Whenever this 'gap' could not be tolerated out by us it would become the moment when an 'identity crisis' takes control over us.

This form of an ailment could be traced as far back as when a witch doctor was around to the present days when we tend to forget whoever we really are.

Although this existing gap has to be around in order to motivate us to head towards an idealistic form our personal image of our own kind of heritage could not be discarded whenever we have to trace our genetic bond.

Therefore our common genetic father has to be remembered regularly since He is the stable bone upon which a universal modem of our form could ever be composed.

His name has to be hailed out properly for if it is being tainted or tampered up, then our heritage could not be directed out in a decent way.

Our genetic ingredients are as important as the existing kinds and therefore we have to survey out this bridge upon daily basis in order to remember our past and look forward over what should become of all of us.

If our past and future have to be brought in the present to inform us who we really are then it follows that a

'Verb' becomes more important than any sort of an 'existing' kind.

This kink should supply us with all the details about our form if we tend to 'apply, project, reflect and convert' it without being inclined to 'look, taste, feel and hear' existing remarks that tomorrow never comes.

Our past has to be brought forth in order to verse out exactly whom we all are.

Over the same logo that had been dictated out before, the same dictum of 'Verbum Factum, Carum, Est' has to be repeated out once again in order to extract an answer about 'who am I'.

Out from the ingredients of that phrase all nature forms could be brought forward to vouch for our identity and from those details information regarding living and not existing becomes apparent to 'us'.

So if we should feel an individual rather than an effigy, we could rise up from amongst the crowd and get down upon our knees and address, 'Our Father, who art in heaven Hallowed be thy Name...... Amen'.

WHERE ARE WE OFF TO?

'To a hospital', is a common answer when the nest is being sought for us to return backwards towards where we had all came out from, before we had arrived here.

'Ashes to ashes and dust to dust' is a universal anagram that could be suitable inscribed out as a common epitaph at the footage of our corpse when the time arrives for us to exit and depart from out of here.

Subsequently a conjunction would normally be inscribed at the dormitory of this scene in order to augur us to remain and stay in 'peace' over at the next place somewhere else.

If our style of 'irony' should be kept at bay and our 'cynical' conduct would refrain from making fun out of what had been just phrased, then this symposium could now proceed and continue along the previous chapter that was left dangling at the end.

Our present human version had previously requested to be kept untouchable from being embroiled into any sort of devious context so as to be eligible to claim a noble title that would be given out to us after we had begged and implored this imaged form to shield and protect us during this terminally phase over here.

This finite aim contains all our future intentions that steers and motivates us all to toil, labor, slave and do whatever is deemed necessary for us to accomplish out an aim which cannot ever be stipulated or expressed out into a logical statement or term over here.

We might conclude that we are doing our best to achieve harmony and tranquility that have never been found out by anyone of us and we are also unable to describe them out as well.

Upon this concept of default we could now embark towards the next stage ahead, and over this prospective twist that only little children perform whenever they could not explain out things precisely we could now explore whatever we are heading for.

Once that we believe into these sorts of tokens that could never be cashed over here then this attitude of innocence could enables us to discover what is shielded out to our clever and intelligent minds that we have.

These sorts of arguments cannot ever be considered to be valued into any rhetoric stance whilst the syllogisms of these logics are flawed in any empiric format exchanged out between us.

However these premises could nowadays be analyzed and rationalized for us to make some sense by modern techniques that have outdated an existing trend of a primitive style of a 'cause and effect' and are now being swiveled upon psychological bench and projected out for us to discover what had not been known before to us.

We had successfully managed to get promoted out from this law of the jungle when we became conscious that this old method of a 'cause and effect' does not get us further more than 'this' and 'that' and so we had inserted a conjunction of an 'if and but' into this equation that was rotated and extended out to present us with more future results out from the past.

This strategic conduct enabled us to trespass over what

we could not see and made us all conscious of things that were impossible for us in the past to believe. Thereupon we had blemished ourselves with a mark of guilt since we had ventured out more than our basic means and our abilities were thus altered and changed into liabilities that could help us to progress or regress back again.

At one side of the coin a guilty conscious had been shed upon us that still haunts our kind whilst on the other hand we were pleased with ourselves that we had flaunted out an existing conduct to be regulated out by us in the future.

We have been blessed out by the phrase of 'peace' and cursed by the burden of an 'onus' that could be spun upon us whenever we open our mouth.

This new fashion enabled us to recognize the meaning of living by governing ourselves through the potentials of existing forms that we got hold of.

Existing forms that have no 'pity, shame, fame or regrets' were being treated out with respect since their diligent methods could never be flawed like the lives we all have.

So a law of the jungle had ended up into an urban mode controlled out by syndicates that were bound with corruptions but were compensated with grief and pity to make good and amend for the mistakes that they incurred.

Human nature had managed to have access towards this nature of a paragon by means of correcting faults and adjusting mistakes that were no longer being just added on or subtracted away, but were currently being divided and multiplied into future problems to be solved whenever a similar need arose.

Floods, fires, earthquakes and beasts that used to cross our paths had supplied us with enough experiences and raw material to practice out more these problems that educated and regulated us to avoid and correct previous types of mistakes.

All these sorts of experiences were consequently being collected out into thoughts and locked up into our memory chamber to be used and utilized for future reference instead of letting them all drifting into 'cause and effect' circulating around in existing forms.

A rotary mode had jammed and changed a cause into a useful net and a situation was projected out into a web of information to help us out whenever we got stuck again.

This new mode had presented us all with opportunities to avoid future mistakes and supplied us with information over which we could be able to chart and plan the next day ahead.

The element of fire and stormy weather must have given us enough material upon which to exercise these prospective conducts that were vital for conceptions and perceptions to be processed upon thought that were spiraling out further more than our organic potentials could afford to understand.

Eventually the element of fire had been controlled and utilized effectively, whilst stormy event must have made us appreciate more the springtime of our lives by the blooming aspect that was enjoyed by the company between us.

This rosy garden had its thorns as well when familiarity was exploited and brought out contempt between us, whilst feeble characters that took longer to mature tried to balance out this anomaly by savaging those who had more possessions than them.

So a dual process that at one point avoided confrontations began to protest to evolve out more and at the other end objections that had no valid reasons to be made had to be condemned.

A breaking point was reached that had copied existence as a model conduct that guaranteed out progress to be reached and achieved, whilst the organic potentials had to submit towards an ideal aspect by means of dialogue.

Perceptions and conceptions presented us with rules and regulations of how far we could stretch our arms or poke our nose into other peoples' lives without being found guilty of breaching existing rules that nature had been justly conducting before we took control of the lives we have.

This was the break of dawn when humanity was made aware that this period of existing was not to be considered out to be the same as living by anyone of us. Along this diagonal process a phrase that augers prosperity and security was composed into the term of 'peace', and at the other end a curse was spun to burden up anyone by the formation of the 'onus' that stains and leave the mark of guilt upon anyone that defies out authority.

These kinds of nature forms still haunts and flaunts our lives under the veils of preachers or solicitors who direct their potentials towards the ligaments of the 'faith' that they profess in their trade.

These diagonal versions had all been based over what we all expect to be done next that could spiral us forward or wind us all backwards towards where we had all came out from before.

Consequently diligent conducts were being awarded a halo of a saint whilst our Mentor was venerated over aspects that were beyond us to understand.

When humanity had reached this illustrious stage, then the bodies of the loved ones were no longer being left out to rot after they had died, but were buried in a dignified manner to prepare them for the journey that they were expected to undertake.

This attitude of expectations presented us with a nature of exploitation and these mysterious episodes injected us with different morals and ethics at every corner that these events were being performed around us.

These different conceptions were thus being applied to assist or persecute out anyone depending upon whether humanity was being more generous and kind or else if people had gone wild or blind again and cannot see what is going to happen out next.

Our elders who at this stage might have became wise could have understood out better what Jesus Christ had meant in chapter 3 of the Gospel of St. John to Nicodemus the priest, whilst at the same time some great rulers who possessed great wealth would have been driven into a dilemma what to do with their means knowing quite well that these tokens would not be valued at the other end, which again an appropriate solution is given out in the Gospel of St. Luke chapter 18 verses 18 – 25 that is very difficult to follow since we all want to go to heaven but none of us would want to die.

These two gospels contain in them the heading and the

footage of our existing span over which a common slab is waiting for all of us but their meanings presents us with hope instead.

This portrait of a new horizon that we all admire from afar, would look ugly if we are asked to donate out all we have to achieve it, and expensive if we have to use our own personal means to be used and utilized by everyone else.

Around and along this dormant trunk of an olive tree could came out leaves that had been nourished from underneath to furnish us with oil that avoids friction whenever we tender our trust towards an ingredient of 'peace'.

The word of 'Peace' might have nowadays lost its former graceful qualities and has been altered and changed out into just plain words of 'hi' or 'hello' but the ingredients are still effective when frigid characters and icy atmospheres becomes friendly and homely whenever this word is being phrased out.

The litmus test that would validate how much we grade this word is given out whenever effort and sacrifices are being tendered out towards those that depends upon us, as well as towards those whom we might not like as much.

This ergonomic term subject us to bow down towards a sacred phrase that could be used to brush away our guilt and guide us all towards where we all wish to go but none of us could describe or locate.

Our human nature never finds it easy to bow down and accepts to be subdued since leadership might be a target that some might pay any price to achieve even if their reputation would be at stake.

Some characters are able to justify out any fault or mistake that they might do, whilst other timid or naïve and honest beings could not be able to waive away a parking ticket that was given to them in the middle of a traffic jam.

All these sorts of slides and tackles are as common upon the legal bench as in any type of sporting events that a ball has to change hands by acrobatic moves that anticipates what is going to happen out next.

These sorts of faults, defaults, gambles and gambits that we conduct or direct are also handled upon a board of chess game that could 'mate, check, trap or snare' a competitor to fall victim and bow down at the end by a master that could plan and program moves ahead by means of perception that anticipates what must happen out next.

Our human nature always keeps on trying to get out more than we actually deserve though we are all conscious and aware that everything over here has to end back into the earth out of which it all had came.

Whenever this stark truth becomes obvious to us, then we become conscious that we had all been worried over a speck of sawdust whilst a plank in front of us had been ignored all the way through.

Although the attitude of 'cause and effect' might have been transformed out into a more advanced stage we might still keep on insisting that the results should always come out exactly to what we had computed out in our mind.

We are all free to think that this attitude of faith, hope, prayers and charity is all a waste of time, money, space and resource that are all useless to us because we have more important issues to attend to.

Once again when any corporation tends to hold these majestic views then the assets of their capital tends to become 'balanced, equated, matched and twinned' up into an audited account, cashed inside a drawer to be taxed again towards another mission to be staged out once more.

Our political nature of a democratic style has advanced us more than a computer which has no sort of an ambition to motivate it to reach another plan that is not in line with the program that had been injected out into its module.

We are all able to 'reflect, project, apply invert' things of the past and conduct them towards the future which is debatable if its exists or not, but the dice that we all hold and the board over which it has to fall are proof enough that we all are living and not just existing if this thrust is transformed out into a trust of faith.

This attitude of grace must be enough proof that someone loves us and cared for all of us before we were even aware of our existing needs that are useful to us but have no pity inside their forms.

All of these tokens that had been donated to us before we had anything to give out in front are proof enough that our lives are precious to someone else who is patiently waiting for us after our potentials all fails us. May our last quest holds a finite aim upon which we all believe is right, just and correct along this valley of sorrows and tears towards:

'Quo Va Dis' = 'Deo Volente @ Tantum Ergo / Amen'.

Lightning Source UK Ltd.
Milton Keynes UK
06 April 2010

152394UK00001B/48/P